Leeds United
Book of Football

LEEDS UNITED
BOOK OF FOOTBALL

With contributions by

DON REVIE
BILLY BREMNER   GARY SPRAKE
JACKIE CHARLTON   NORMAN HUNTER
PAUL REANEY   EDDIE GRAY   MICK JONES
JOHNNY GILES   PAUL MADELEY
PETER LORIMER   MICK O'GRADY
TERRY COOPER   ROD BELFITT
KEITH ARCHER

Souvenir Press

© Copyright 1969 Leeds United Football Club Ltd.
All rights reserved

First published 1969 by Souvenir
Press Ltd., 95 Mortimer Street,
London, W.1, and simultaneously
by The Ryerson Press, Toronto 2,
Canada

*No part may be reproduced in any form
without permission in writing from the
publisher except for a reviewer who
wishes to quote brief passages for the
purposes of a review.*

SBN.285.50265.4

Printed in Great Britain by
The Northumberland Press Limited
Gateshead

Contents

	FOREWORD	9
1	DON REVIE A Case of Teamwork through and through	13
2	If at First you Don't succeed . . .	22
3	GARY SPRAKE My debut made me sick	39
4	PAUL REANEY Local Boy—from Fulham—makes good	44
5	TERRY COOPER The Day Alan Ball had me 'tickled pink'	47
6	PAUL MADELEY I don't care where 'the Boss' plays me	52
7	BILLY BREMNER I'm a meek and mild character, really	55
8	JACKIE CHARLTON I was a one-man awkward Squad	61
9	NORMAN HUNTER Snap, Crackle and Pop	70
10	He's United's No. 1 Supporter	74
11	High Drama in Europe	77
12	Final Triumph in Budapest	87
13	MICK O'GRADY The Luckiest Day in my Life	96

14	JOHNNY GILES	
	The Lessons I learned at Leeds	100
15	MICK JONES	
	Goals are My Business	105
16	EDDIE GRAY	
	Never Mind my Dad, Leeds are 'tops'	111
17	PETER LORIMER	
	The Night 'the Boss' was caught Speeding	115
18	ROD BELFITT	
	Those G.C.E. exams were worth it	119
19	Split pants knocked United out of the Cup	121
20	KEITH ARCHER	
	The Team behind the Team	124
21	Elland Road Academy	127
22	The Moment of Truth	143

Illustrations

	FACING PAGE
Leeds United	32
Leeds United chairman, Alderman P. A. Woodward	33
Bobby Collins shows his F.A. Cup runners-up Medal to the Lord Mayor of Leeds after the 1965 final	33
Peter Lorimer scores a goal in the fourth round of the F.A. Cup in 1967	64
Was it a goal?	64
Albert Johanneson scores the first goal in the third round F.A. Cup replay last season	65
Sheffield Wednesday score the equaliser in the third round F.A. Cup game at Hillsborough	65

BETWEEN PAGES 80 AND 81

Don Revie and Bertie Mee lead out their teams for the League Cup final at Wembley

Billy Bremner introduces Don Revie to Princess Alexandra before the League Cup Final

Billy Bremner holds the Football League Cup in triumph on the steps of the Leeds Civic Hall

The goal which brought Leeds United their first major honour

The late Albert Morris, Terry Cooper, Billy Bremner and Don Revie with the Football League Cup

A good example of Leeds United defence

ILLUSTRATIONS

BETWEEN PAGES 80 AND 81

Johnny Giles takes a penalty kick

Rod Belfitt scores one of United's goals during the F.A. Cup second replay against Sunderland

The final whistle has gone and Rod Belfitt needs treatment for cramp

	FACING PAGE
The Leeds United team off on yet another trip abroad	96
Mick O'Grady gets the winner against Manchester United in last season's League game	96
The Elland Road ground under reconstruction	97
Don Revie and Keith Archer with the backroom staff	97
The late Albert Morris congratulates members of the Dinamo Zagreb team on their winning of the 1967 Fairs Cup	128
Billy Bremner rejoices on scoring the winning goal against Standard Liege	128
Mick Jones scores the goal which brought the Inter-Cities Fairs Cup to Leeds	129
The moment of triumph—the Inter-Cities Fairs Cup at last comes to Leeds	129

Photographs are acknowledged to Yorkshire Post Newspapers Ltd., Manchester Daily Mail and Scottish Daily Express

Foreword

By Leeds United chairman Alderman Percy Woodward

As your chairman, I am proud to present to you the Leeds United Book of Football. For us, it is a new venture—and we hope it will become an annual publication, to put on record the inside story of what we believe will be continued success in both British and European football.

Let me say right from the start that the book is for YOU. Our aim is to put you right in the picture behind the scenes at Elland-road—and to keep you in the picture. We hope it will be of real interest to you all.

Our successes in the past few years have been magnificent by any standards, and there is no one prouder than myself that, after so many years in the wilderness, we have now, under the shrewd guidance of our manager, Don Revie, and his loyal and hard-working backroom boys—and girls—given you something to shout about.

It has been by concentrating on youth and team spirit that we have won our way from the very depths of the Second Division to the top of the First Division tree. And while this book may be aimed at the younger element of our faithful fans, we believe that there is something for everyone in it.

I am sure that our older supporters who, as I do, remember the darker days at Elland-road, will find plenty to interest them and to increase their pride in the club.

We want you to have the best—both on the field, and off it—and from chairman to our youngest apprentice we are constantly working towards that aim.

You are just as much a part of the team which is Leeds United as the board of directors or the players.

Your encouragement and support can be vital in the hectic days which, we hope, lie ahead. We want you to feel that you 'belong' to the great big happy family at Elland-road. And if this book helps to strengthen the link between club and supporters, it will have achieved its object.

PERCY WOODWARD

Leeds United
Book of Football

1. *A Case of Teamwork through and through*

DON REVIE

IN A PLAYING career with five clubs—Hull City, Leicester City, Leeds United, Manchester City and Sunderland—I learned a lot about the joys and the heartaches of professional football. I knew the rocky road a team must tread in its battle against relegation; I knew the champagne feeling of going to Wembley for an F.A. Cup final. But, as I discovered when I landed my first managerial job, with Leeds, I didn't know the half of it!

Crossing over the fence from player to manager can be a very tricky business. You are suddenly 'the boss'—although you don't know if all your former team-mates will accept you as such, so swiftly. You have to try to be a players' man, still—yet earn their respect for your authority. And the switch can be all the more difficult, when you find yourself in charge of a club whose fortunes are low. And I must thank Mr Harry Reynolds, the chairman at that time, and the board, not only for the opportunity, but also for the help—help which they have continued to give me all the time with the minimum of interference.

I have been the manager of Leeds United now for eight years—eight years, on which I can look back and pinpoint the highlights and the low spots. And there have been plenty of both, I will confess. But let me say, straight at the outset, that the success we have achieved increasingly, season by season, has been no one-man job. It has been a case of teamwork through and through—and that means off the field, as well as on it.

A manager is only as good as his team. That means the backroom team, as well as the eleven players who go out on the park every Saturday. I got a tremendous lot of help and encouragement in the early days from our former chairman, Harry Reynolds and from Cyril Williamson who was then General-manager; I also have been helped terrifically by the backroom team who work unceasingly for Leeds, Syd Owen, Les Cocker, Maurice Lindley, Bob English and Cyril Partridge and company ... what we have achieved couldn't have been done without their aid—and their loyalty. There was a time when Syd Owen, for example, could have landed an extremely good job with Tottenham Hotspur; instead, he chose to stay at Ellandroad, because he believed in the work we were doing, and he wanted to be there when we reaped the benefit from it all. I have little doubt, too, that Les Cocker—he *is* the team trainer of the England Under-23 team and assistant to Harold Shepherdson for the Senior squad, remember —and others in the backroom team could have found themselves good jobs elsewhere; but they have stayed, too. They started a job, and they wanted to finish it.

Now we are coming up to our best years—and I say this, in spite of the fact that we have already won the League championship, the Football League Cup and the Inter-Cities Fairs Cup. But we have still some way to go before we can sit back and say: 'Now we are satisfied ...' In fact, I doubt if we shall *ever* be able to sit back and say that. But I believe there *will* come a day when we have landed the F.A. Cup ... *and* the European Cup. Maybe, even the world-club championship. Until then, we shall continue to work towards these goals.

But before I set out our ambitions—and, believe me, we *have* ambitions at Leeds—let's do a little bit of recapping on all that has gone before ... right back to the time I first sat in the managerial chair. The fortunes of the club were pretty low. I was a new boy—new to the very complex business of management itself. I needed help and guidance, and I wasn't too proud to turn to people in the game who possessed the knowledge which, I felt sure, could help me.

Those were days of anxiety, believe me. For I knew that we were far from being even a Second Division promotion force—indeed, we were perilously near the brink of relegation to the *Third* Division. We had some good youngsters coming up, but time was not on our side. So we had to buy. My first major signing, of course, was wee Bobby Collins, from Everton—and, at £25,000, what a bargain he turned out to be! Almost from the day he arrived at Elland-road, we started to move forward.

Of course, Bobby didn't do it all by himself; everyone pitched in to do his best for the club. And together, the lot of us began to weld a tremendous team spirit which has remained—and played no small part in our surge through to success. We didn't go down—and we started, slowly, to ascend the Second Division table. We finished fifth from the top, and, had we had a less disastrous start to the season, I am convinced we would have skated into the First Division. But the following season, we carried on from where we had left off, and we *did* emerge from the Second Division as champions. I was satisfied ... up to a point. I knew we were good enough to hold our own in the top flight, but even I was surprised (a little, anyway) when we finished runners-up for the title. We were hard on the heels of the leaders almost all the way through the season, and we were really pipped on the post—by goal average.

You may recall that we went for the League and F.A. Cup double; Manchester United just edged us out of the title (despite our grandstand finish in the final game at Birmingham) and Liverpool took the F.A. Cup, but only after the Wembley final had gone to extra time. Our consolation was that Bobby Collins was named 'Player of the Year', and that he, Billy Bremner and Jackie Charlton were called up for international duty by Scotland and England respectively.

The next season, we were trying for a double top again —this time, the League and the Inter-Cities Fairs Cup. Again, we were edged out of the honours. Then, the following season, we went for a three-timer—League, F.A. Cup and Inter-Cities Fairs Cup. We hung on to the bitter end, and it *was* the bitter end, because we finished up once again with nothing to show for our efforts.

So, as well as having won the reputation of being a hard team to beat, we were rapidly acquiring a reputation as the team which finished second-best ... the team of champion runners-up. But last time out, it was a different story, because we were back at Wembley for the League Cup final against Arsenal, and a goal by left-back Terry Cooper —the only goal of the game—brought the trophy back to Leeds. For the first time, we had some silverware to put on the sideboard and display to admiring visitors. We even went one better, having finally won something—we collected the Fairs Cities Cup, for good measure. So, season by season, we have proved consistent, and a real threat to every other aspirant for honours, no matter whether it was in the League, the F.A. Cup, the League Cup or in Europe.

Now, you don't achieve such consistency purely because luck is on your side. You achieve it because you have groomed and produced players of a high calibre—players who can slot into the first team as if they had been playing there all their lives. Our average age, around that time, was about 24; and I said then that I would like to see these players when they had added a couple of years' experience to their play. *Then*, I believed, we would really get the measure of our true ability.

Only a season or two ago we did tremendously well, even though we were plagued by injuries. For example, at one stage we had made about 180 changes, just through injury; we had Johnny Giles out of action for a month—and Johnny suffered a bit through injury in the first half of last season, as well—and we had players like Jackie Charlton and Mike O'Grady on the sidelines. In fact, during that spell, we were without our two recognised wingers right from the Christmas. So we couldn't really have a settled team ... yet the youngsters who were drafted in, through this emergency, played their part in helping to keep us among the challengers for honours.

We owe a tremendous debt to our scouts—the men who go out in all kinds of weather, and stand along the touch-line vetting potential Soccer talent. Our scouts, indeed, have ensured that Leeds United have had a steady supply of the best young talent in Britain—which, in turn, has provided us with players who have graduated through to the first team, and saved hundreds of thousands of pounds in transfer expenditure.

At the same time, we have not been afraid to speculate in the transfer market—and, while we have not spent as much as some other clubs, we have paid hefty fees for star players who, we felt, would fit into the Leeds United pattern. We sold the legendary John Charles to Italy—and re-signed him; we also transferred him again, and still managed to make a profit on the deal.

We paid more than £50,000 for Alan Peacock; but, unfortunately, injury problems didn't really enable club or player to get the return we might have hoped. Alan scored some vital goals for us in our early promotion days, and he was always giving 100 per cent effort—he deserved a far better break from the Soccer fates, in fact.

Johnny Giles was an acquisition from Manchester United, and how well he assumed the mantle of Bobby Collins when the wee Scot finally left Elland-road. We went to Huddersfield for winger Mike O'Grady—and only now, really, are we seeing the best of Mike, who had a real struggle to overcome injury troubles during his earlier days at Leeds.

And we went to another Yorkshire club, Sheffield United, for centre-forward Mick Jones. He cost Leeds United £100,000, and he has been repaying that fantastic outlay, game by game, with the goals he has scored and the weight he has taken off other players in the attack.

But the fact remains that most of our team *is* home-produced, and when you look at the players who have won international honours, you will soon realise what a fine all-round side we have. There is hardly a man in Leeds United's first-team squad who hasn't won some representative honour or other.

I have tried never to forget, and always to remember (which is a slightly different thing), the words which Harry Reynolds said to me, when I was given the job of manager. In any business, he informed me, management was common sense, and the courage to apply it. He added that the hardest part of achieving success was living up to it. I have come to realise that this is indeed so.

Now, Leeds United have been involved in plenty of thrillers in the past few seasons—any team challenging for honours has some tremendous battles against its rivals, at home and in Europe. We have faced the best in Britain and on the Continent, and we have come well out of the exchanges. We have had our strokes of fortune—such as winning the flip of a disc, to decide the winners of a European tie. A situation I have never relished, for tossing a coin or flipping a disc to decide the winners of a game is farcical, in my view.

We have also had our hard times—the game when Bobby Collins broke a leg in Turin, the battle against Napoli last season, for example. And we have had our great games and our moments of disappointment. But I don't believe any of our supporters can say that Leeds United have failed to give them value for money. And I say that sincerely.

It has, therefore, been a source of some sadness to me that we have not had bigger gates at Elland-road. If Arthur

Dunhill can travel the length and breadth of Britain—and Europe—to support his favourite team, surely the people in Leeds can come down to Elland-road on a Saturday or a Wednesday night? When we played Hanover, for instance, in the Fairs Cities Cup last season, only 24,000 turned up to see us score five goals. I know it was a bitter night ... but if that game had gone on at Old Trafford, there would have been a 63,000 full house!

Now let me hasten to add that we *do* appreciate the support we get from true-blue Leeds fans. The folk who do come down to Elland-road let us know they are there, all right, with their lusty cheers. But to the people who have been giving us a miss, I would just like to say that we *are* recognised as being one of the best teams in Europe, and we *have* erased that unwanted tag of being the best runners-up in the business. So, please, will you give us a trial in the new season? I think we've earned that much ... and, after all, if you don't like what you see, you can always decide to stay home next time.

Believe me, the need for continuing, and increased, support is vital. Why? *Let me spell it out to you now.*

I believe that we can justly say our progress on the Soccer fields of Britain and abroad has been remarkable, in the past eight seasons, but I want us to go on even further. We *were* a second-rate footballing power, if you like; but now we have proved that we can share top billing with most clubs, on ability, and we want to attain the status which signals, for the whole of the footballing world to see, that we are *The Best of All*. To do that, of course, it costs money, as well as effort. And so the support from the fans can play a vital role in our ambitions—ambitions which are spread over the next four or five years.

Yes, we have done pretty well in eight seasons; but there is another goal ahead. Since I became the manager of Leeds United, and I don't take all the credit for what I am going to say next, we have wiped out a debt of a quarter of a million pounds. Just roll that sum around in your head, figure out what £250,000 means ... and you will realise the magnitude of the sum—and the task.

Add to that the fact that when you take ground improvements and signings into account, we have *spent* close on half a million pounds, and you will come to realise what a gigantic money-spinning sport this little old game of Soccer has become. It's not an insular game now; it's a world-wide game. And we've got to go on and on.

We have several targets, bracketed together. I want Leeds United to win the F.A. Cup. Even more, now we have won the First Division championship we want to take on the cream of Europe's footballing talent—and *beat* them. In other words, I want the European Cup to stand on the sideboard at Elland-road. And, if possible, I want us to go on from there and do what Glasgow Celtic and Manchester United failed to do ... land the world club championship. I also want Leeds United to attain the *Status* which Manchester United enjoy in the eyes of the footballing public ... of the whole, wide Soccer world, not just Britain.

We have switched our style somewhat, because now I believe we have got the players to win matches by scoring goals, rather than win them by keeping the opposition out. We can afford to be more fluid in our style of play; still tight at the back, when necessary, but more adventurous up front. That way, we will be a more entertaining side to watch, and we shall still be collecting the points that matter so much.

We are certainly a fine all-round side—there isn't a Soccer judge in the world who would dispute that statement. But I won't rest content until Leeds United are acknowledged to be a *great* side, fit to rank alongside the Real Madrids, the Benficas and the Manchester Uniteds.

When I first came into this game as a manager, I turned to Sir Matt Busby for advice, on more than one occasion. He was the manager I admired most; his club was the one above all others which was worth emulating. United carried a glamour and a pulling power all on its own. There was—and still is—a brand of magnetism about the names of Sir Matt Busby and Manchester United which breed admiration.

I want Leeds United to be bracketed in the same breath as Manchester United. I believe it may take us three or four more years to achieve this—*but I believe it can be done*. And when we do reach this particular goal, I want the name of Leeds United to be compared with that of Manchester United in every way—on the field and off it. I want Leeds United to be able to match Manchester United on all counts.

I want us to have won everything in sight; to be a magnetic drawing card whenever and wherever we play. In fact, I want us to be even *better* than anyone else. It will take some doing, but I believe we are on the way to reaching our ultimate goal. With the players we have today, the players who are coming through in the junior teams, the backroom staff we have welded into such a formidable team—and the same team spirit which has taken us to our successes, so far.

2. If at First you Don't succeed . . .

A COUPLE OF seasons ago, Leeds United wing-half Norman Hunter set up an individual endurance record for an English professional footballer, when he played 71 games in the season. But United themselves have bid fair to claim some sort of endurance record as a club.

Always, it seems, it has been a case of 'If at first you don't succeed, try, try, try again'. United kicked off in the Second Division, in season 1920–21, and finished 14th, with 38 points. The same number of points the following season saw them move up to eighth place, and the season after that, they finished seventh, with 47 points. Then came promotion, in season 1923–24, when they finished in first place, with 54 points. Exactly 40 years were to go by before they had anything else really to cheer about.

The first flush of promotion success was rapidly cooled—United's first season in the top flight was not an easy one, and they finished 18th spot in the table, having gathered 34 points. The next season, with two points more, they had slipped down one position, and the next season, with only 30 points, they had dropped to 21st in the table. So it was back to the Second Division.

Back they bounced, at the end of season 1927–28, as Second Division runners-up, with 57 points. Forty-one points saw them finish a respectable 13th in the First

Division table, the following term, and they shot up to fifth place, with 46 points, the season after that.

The next season, 1930–31, it was the same old story ... down they shot to finish 21st, with 31 points, and the Second Division was their destination once more. Again United bounced straight back, though, finishing second in season 1931–32, with 54 points—and this time they stayed in the top flight for eight years. But they did nothing spectacular in that time ... they finished eighth (44 points), ninth (42), 18th (38), 11th (41), 19th (34), 9th again (43), 13th (41) ... and then came the humiliation of finishing bottom team of all, with a mere 18 points to their credit.

That was the start of a promotion campaign which took *nine* seasons to achieve success. Indeed, in season 1947–48, their first term back in the Second Division, they came perilously close to dropping into the Third Division, for they finally finished 18th, with only 36 points. It was a close call, indeed. The season after that, United managed to climb to 15th spot, with 37 points—and then, for two successive seasons, they were fifth in the table, with 47 and 48 points respectively.

The indications were that United could stage a promotion revival, and the hopes of their supporters began to grow. In season 1951–52, United slipped a place, to sixth, but there was still a good chance that they would do even better the following term. After all, fifth, fifth and sixth indicated consistency of the right sort.

Disappointment came in season 1952–53, though, when Leeds United dropped from sixth to tenth, and it was in that position that they finished their campaign the following season, as well.

Season 1954–55 saw United regain their momentum, when they soared into fourth place, with 53 points, and although they finished the following term with one point fewer, their total of 52 was sufficient to see them emerge from the Second Division once more as runners-up.

The progress was maintained in that first term back in

Division 1 Soccer, for they climbed the table and completed the season in a very creditable eighth position, with 44 points—just as they had done in their first season after promotion in 1932. However, 1957–58 saw them in a more familiar position, for they dropped to 17th, having mustered 37 points, and then they climbed two more places to finish 15th, with 39 points the following season. But worse was to come, for the club and its long-suffering supporters ... for in season 1959–60, United had slumped once more, to 21st place in the table. Their scanty haul of 34 points ensured that they dropped into the Second Division once more.

United's first two seasons in the lower grade was far from spectacular—instead of bouncing straight back, as their supporters had hoped, they finished 14th in the table, with 38 points, then dropped to 19th, with 36 points. Don Revie had stepped up from player to manager, and he had taken over at a critical time. But although football was not to know it just then, that placing of 19th was really the start of a tremendous upsurge which saw United shoot back into the First Division and become a real footballing power in the land. From the perils of relegation in season 1961–62, United recovered to stage a drive which took them ever onwards and upwards.

In season 1962–63, United climbed up and up, after a terrible start, and finished in fifth place. The whole mood of the club had altered, and there was optimism in the air, backed by the knowledge that United had a team of young players who could go places. First Division places, they hoped.

That optimism was not misplaced, either, for season 1963–64 saw United emerge into the First Division spotlight again, this time as Second Division champions, with 63 points—a total never before achieved by the club.

And straight away, the 'new' Leeds United continued to set Soccer tongues wagging throughout the country, as they shot higher and higher in the First Division table. It was a season's end of drama, a real cliffhanger, as United battled it out with their Manchester counterparts for the honour of finishing First Division champions. The last game of the season decided matters, and Leeds United were the ones who finished disappointed, for although they had piled up a massive total of 61 First Division points, they had to be content with second place.

The years of hope and near-disaster, of disappointment and almost total disillusion, were long, hard years of endurance. That 1964–65 season, when Leeds United finished runners-up, was the start of another endurance serial ... although, this time, the near-misses and the disappointments were tinged with consolation—consolation that, at last, here was a Leeds United team which could not be lightly dismissed, whenever and wherever honours were being sought, at the highest level in the game.

In the League Leeds United achieved a tremendous record of consistency, while still winning nothing, when the honours were distributed. They finished second, second, fourth and fourth, and were engaged in a season-long battle last term with Liverpool, Everton and Arsenal before they won the elusive title they had sought so long.

Since their return to the First Division, United have never finished with fewer than 53 points, and at the start of every term, the bookmakers have made them a short-priced bet to win the First Division championship, not to mention the League Cup, the F.A. Cup and the Inter-Cities Fairs Cup—more about which later. Indeed, the bookies knew and respected United's form so much that barely two seasons ago, they quoted them at 17–1 to win the League, the F.A. Cup and the Inter-Cities Fairs Cup. It was a fantastic treble, and a staggeringly short price, but, even so, Leeds proved that the bookies knew what they were doing, for they came tremendously close to pulling off all three, being in the race to the bitter end.

But even if it seemed like the bitter end, when United realised that they would collect none of these trophies, it was almost the final stage in the great endurance test. For after a failure in the Fairs Cup final against Dinamo Zagreb, United went on to collect the Football League Cup and the Inter-Cities Fairs Cup, so that *two* trophies stood alongside each other on the sideboard.

Some folk have said that Leeds have tried to win too much, at once. Manager Don Revie does not go along with that. 'I realise that 60 or 70 games in one season is a terrific burden to place upon players, in the highly competitive professional game of today,' he says. 'But it is *Because* the game is so fiercely competitive that you *Must* go all-out for everything. Our players are trained and tuned to last the pace, even if every game is like a cup-tie.

'It took Manchester United 12 seasons of trying, to win the European Cup. We at Leeds know that we must go on trying, game after game, season after season—*it's the only way.*

'And now that we have tasted success, we are looking for other honours to add to our list. For instance, we have done nothing in the F.A. Cup—and I'm not dismissing our Wembley appearance against Liverpool in 1965. And we have yet to play in the European Cup. These are things which we *shall* taste in the future.'

United's record in the F.A. Cup has been a pretty dismal one, in fact. Going back to 1922, when they first played in the competition, they have reached Wembley but once.

In 1922, they lost 2–1 at Swindon in the first round. A season later, after having beaten Portsmouth, they drew, no score, at Fratton Park, and won the replay 3–1, United went out in round two at Bolton, by 3–1.

After a 1–0 victory at home against Stoke in 1924, hopes were raised when United drew 1–1 at West Ham, won the replay 1–0, and tackled Aston Villa away in the third round. The hopes were short lived—Villa scored three goals, United failed to score, and the third round ended United's interest in the competition.

In 1925, United were out, first go—thrashed 3–0 at

IF AT FIRST YOU DON'T SUCCEED... 27

Anfield; in 1926, they were hammered 5–1 at Middlesbrough; and after beating Sunderland 3–2 at Elland-road in 1927, they could do no better than draw, 0–0, at home to Bolton ... and they went down at Burnden Park by three clear goals.

Manchester City saw off Leeds United, by the only goal of the game at Maine-road, in 1928; in 1929, United travelled down to Exter, drew 2–2, and won the Elland-road replay 5–1. Once more, hopes began to rise, but Yorkshire neighbours and rivals Huddersfield dashed those hopes with a 2–0 victory at Leeds-road in the next round.

Came 1930, and Crystal Palace crashed to an ignominious 8–1 defeat at Elland-road ... then Leeds crashed themselves, to another United. This time it was West Ham who ran out 4–1 winners at Upton Park.

Leeds gained their revenge over Huddersfield in 1931, when they met and beat them, 2–0, at Elland-road; then Leeds disposed of Newcastle, 4–1, in a home tie; but they went down, 3–1, at Exeter in the next round. And in 1932, Queen's Park Rangers defeated United 3–1.

Came 1933, and Newcastle were on the receiving end of a 3–0 thrashing at Elland-road; Leeds drew no score at Tranmere in the next round, and won the replay 4–0. But another Merseyside team, Everton, polished off Leeds by two goals to nil at Goodison, so the fifth round was the final one for Leeds. And in 1934, Preston travelled to Elland-road, kept United at bay, and scored a lone goal to put paid to United's hopes of a Cup run that year.

Yorkshire rivals Bradford travelled the short distance to Elland-road in 1935—and went home 4–1 losers; then Leeds made the long haul to East Anglia to visit Norwich, came back with a 3–3 draw ... and lost their home replay 2–1.

The year 1936 saw United make some progress as they drew 1–1 at Molineux, and disposed of the Wolves by three goals to one in the Elland-road replay. Then United played Bury at home, and were winning 2–1 when fog came down and the game was abandoned. United and Bury met again, and Leeds scored three goals out of the five which were recorded. But Yorkshire rivals Sheffield United put an end to further progress, when they won the Bramall-lane encounter 3–1.

In 1937, United travelled to Stamford Bridge, and were summarily dumped out of the Cup by Chelsea, who won 4–0. A year later, United beat Chester 3–1 at Elland-road ... then it was down to The Valley, where Charlton ran out 2–1 winners. In 1939, United beat Bournemouth 3–1 at home—and lost 4–2 on the same ground to Huddersfield. Mercifully, in the view of many United followers, the war intervened and ended the F.A. Cup-ties.

The third-round tie between United and Middlesbrough in 1946 proved a humdinger—the teams drew 4–4 at Elland-road, then Boro' went on to score a crushing 7–2 victory at Ayresome. For three successive seasons, after that, United never went further than the third round— they lost 2–1 at West Brom, 4–0 at Blackpool, and 3–1 at home to little Newport County. Days of disaster, indeed. But 1950 looked a much better year, until the sixth round.

United started off by beating Carlisle away, 5–2; they drew 1–1 at home to Bolton, disposed of them 3–2 in the Burnden replay; they defeated Cardiff 3–1 at Elland-road ... and then lost to Arsenal at Highbury by the only goal of the match. Still, they *had* reached the sixth round.

Stern tasks were ahead, too, for in 1951 United defeated Middlesbrough 1–0 at Elland-road, then went to Old Trafford and took a 4–0 drubbing. In 1952, lowly Rochdale tackled United at Spotland, and went down 2–0. United scored twice again, to defeat Bradford at Elland-road, then ran up against Chelsea once more. This time it was a marathon duel. At Elland-road, the teams finished level, 1–1; they did the same at Stamford Bridge; and then, at Villa Park, Chelsea broke the deadlock in no uncertain manner by scoring five goals to United's one. That's the Cup.

From 1953 to 1962, Leeds United never progressed

beyond the third round of the competition, and their *bête noire* turned out to be Cardiff City. It started with a third-round trip to Brentford in 1953—and the London club won, 2-1. In 1954, an Elland-road draw (3-3) against Tottenham was followed by a 1-0 defeat at White Hart-lane, and in 1955, Torquay took up the cudgels. They drew 2-2 at Elland-road, and cruised home, 4-0, in the replay. Enter Cardiff...

For *three* successive seasons, Leeds United and Cardiff City were paired with each other in the third round of the F.A. Cup. *Three* times, and on every occasion, Leeds were favoured with the home draw. The first time Cardiff travelled to Elland-road, in 1956, they won 2-1; the following season, they won by exactly the same score; and the season after that, they made it a treble ... by 2-1 again. No wonder Cardiff were happy to be drawn against United, even away; no wonder United began to fear the very mention of Cardiff's name. If ever there were a bogy team, Cardiff were the one!

Leeds were laughing their heads off, when they learned that they had been drawn against Luton, in 1959. United were away, but anything was better than coming up against Cardiff once more ... so they thought. When Luton had scored five, against a lone goal from United, even Cardiff didn't seem such terrible opposition, after all.

The same old story of failure continued. In 1960, United lost 2-1 at Villa Park; in 1961, they lost 2-0 to Sheffield Wednesday, at Hillsborough. Then the skies cleared a little as 1963 saw United get beyond the third round for the first time in years. They demolished Stoke 3-1 at Elland-road, went to Middlesbrough and won 2-0—then crashed 3-0 away to Nottingham Forest.

And in 1964, they were drawn against ... Cardiff City. This time, at Ninian Park. United returned laughing, for a change—they had scored the only goal of the game, and so gained a little of their own back for those three successive defeats Cardiff had inflicted on them at Elland-road.

After Cardiff, it was Everton, at home, and United could do no better than draw, 1–1. In the Goodison replay, they didn't score at all, while Everton got two.

Then came the season which is still recalled with joy and despair ... the season when, at long last, after 40 years of trying, Leeds United hit the Wembley trail. It began, inauspiciously enough, with a visit from little Southport. Leeds won that encounter, 3–0. The fourth round, as had happened the season before, Everton were the visitors to Elland-road—and again, it was a 1–1 draw. United followers, recalling what had happened last time, hoped for the best, but feared the worst. At Goodison, though, it was a glory night, after all. 'Ilkla' Moor' rang out, as United won, 2–1.

Another team from the lower grade made their appearance at Elland-road in round five—Shrewsbury Town came, saw—and were conquered, 2–0. By this time, the United players were beginning to get the scent of Wembley in their nostrils.

The sixth-round tie against Crystal Palace was played in the depths of a bitter winter, and United finally ran out 3–0 winners. And so to the semi-finals, which paired United with their Manchester counterparts, at Hillsborough. It saw Leeds forward Johnny Giles in opposition to his old team, including his brother-in-law, Nobby Stiles. And it saw a game ruined by the muddy conditions, with neither team able to master them, or score a goal.

The replay was at the City Ground, Nottingham; and again, it looked like being a deadlock, as the teams battled away to break each other's defensive barrier. Finally, it was Johnny Giles who sent the ball over for Billy Bremner to head into Manchester United's net. There was barely time to kick off again, and it was all over. Leeds United, for the first time in their history, were at Wembley. And there they met Liverpool.

It is history, now, of course, how the teams played for 90 minutes without either side having scored a decisive goal; history how, finally, Liverpool managed to pierce their opponents' defence during extra time, and, even though Leeds came back into the game with a goal, ran out 2–1 winners. Defeat was a bitter anti-climax for Leeds United's efforts, but as manager Don Revie said: 'This isn't the end of the world. We have suffered disappointments before, and we shall suffer them again. But we will have our triumphs, too.'

Leeds could look back upon a season of tremendous endeavour, even if it were tinged with failure at the final hurdles. But they did finish knowing that they had earned a high all-round praise for their skills and their efforts ... and in wee Bobby Collins, they had the man who was voted Player of the Year.

The year 1966 saw Leeds once more on the honours trail, but in the F.A. Cup they did not get beyond the fourth round. Drawn at home to Bury in the third, they made no mistake, and the Shakers went home shattered, after their 6–1 hammering. But United drew a really tough nut in round four, and they found it just too hard to crack. Chelsea, managed by Tommy Docherty then, were going great guns themselves, and at Stamford Bridge they just scraped through, by the only goal of the game. The following season, the two teams met again—this time in a semi-final at Villa Park.

For Leeds, 1967 kicked off with a home draw against Crystal Palace, one of the teams they had beaten on their way to Wembley two years earlier. They defeated Palace 3–0, and took on West Brom at Elland-road. There were plenty of folk who said they would not be surprised to see West Brom pull off one of the day's shock victories, for the Throstles were emerging as a side with a reputation for upsetting the odds. But on the day, United came good and sank West Brom without trace—the 5–0 margin told its own story.

The fifth round was a far-from-easy tie—away to Sunderland. Leeds didn't surmount this hurdle at the first time of asking, but they managed to get a 1-1 draw, and felt confident they could do the rest at Elland-road. Sunderland, however, proved a surprise packet, and after the second game, the scores were again 1-1, which meant a replay at Boothferry Park, Hull. After 90 minutes there, Sunderland were on their way home—and out. For although they had scored, Leeds had got two.

The sixth round was another tremendous battle, this time at Elland-road, against Manchester City, who were being steered towards a First Division championship by Joe Mercer and Malcolm Allison, although at that time, of course, no one knew this. City still claim that they were unfortunate not to get even a replay, but the scoreline records that Leeds notched the only goal of the game. And so it was on to a semi-final against Chelsea, at Villa Park—a semi-final staged by two of the best, two of the fittest teams in the land.

Chelsea manager Tommy Docherty had gone to Aston Villa for a centre-forward, and Tony Hateley cost him £100,000. 'The Doc', had emerged with a reputation which marked him down as a good manager, and a controversial one. He signed, he sold; he wanted Chelsea to succeed in a hurry. And when he signed Tony Hateley, it was another controversial move. But at the end of that semi-final, it was 'The Doc', who was doing the victory jig, 'The Doc', who was saying: 'That's what's I bought Hateley for—the £100,000 goal.' For it was Hateley who scored, and that goal took Chelsea to a Wembley final against Tottenham. But there are a lot of Leeds fans who still reckon United should have had at least a replay when Peter Lorimer, late in the game, lashed the ball into Chelsea's net following a Johnny Giles freekick. It looked a good goal but the referee disallowed it—and he is the man who counts!

Once more, then, Leeds finished up being the losers. Once more, they gritted their teeth, and looked forward, instead of looking back with regret. Once more they hit

BACK ROW left to right: Paul Madeley, Mick O'Grady, David Harvey, Gary Sprake, Jack Charlton, Norman Hunter. MIDDLE ROW: Albert Johanneson, Rod Belfitt, Mick Jones, Terry Hibbitt, Eddie Gray, Peter Lorimer, Don Revie (manager). FRONT ROW: Paul Reaney, Terry Cooper, Johnny Giles, Billy Bremner, Jimmy Greenhoff (now Birmingham City), Mick Bates, Les Cocker (chief trainer-coach).

Leeds United chairman, Alderman P. A. Woodward.

Plenty of smiles, but this was not such a happy occasion as Bobby Collins, *right*, shows his F.A. Cup runners-up medal to the Lord Mayor of Leeds, Alderman Mrs. L. Naylor, after Liverpool had beaten them 2–1 in the 1965 final at Wembley.

the F.A. Cup trail, and in the 1968 term, their third-round opponents turned out to be Derby County. Derby visited Elland-road, and departed, 2-0 victims.

It was a remarkable Cup draw for Leeds last year, in fact, because they played every game bar one on their own ground—and the exception was the semi-final against Everton. For the third season out of four, Leeds reached the semi-final stages of the competition—proof, if such were needed, that they had reached the stage where they were *almost* unbeatable. Almost...

Nottingham Forest followed Derby as the fourth-round visitors to Elland-road, and they, too went home trying to forget their sorrows, after Leeds had won 2-1. Bristol City were United's next opponents, and this time it was a 2-0 victory for Leeds. In the sixth round, two Yorkshire clubs were paired—Leeds United versus Sheffield United—and the Blades had a very good Cup-fighting record indeed. But when it was all over, back they went to Sheffield, leaving Leeds laughing as 1-0 winners. Which meant that United would travel for the first time—to Old Trafford, for their semi-final against Everton.

Anyone who was there that day will recall that it was a fine game. Everton's young thoroughbreds, groomed by Harry Catterick and his backroom team, were just beginning to make a real impact on First Division Soccer. Since they had won the League championship in the early 1960's, Everton had acquired new players, and blooded other youngsters. They had been to Wembley a couple of seasons earlier, and triumphed 3-2 in a dramatic game against Sheffield Wednesday. Everton, two goals down at one stage, had snatched victory from apparent defeat, even as the Everton supporters were starting to vent their disappointment on Harry Catterick, who had left out Fred Pickering and gambled on Mike Trebilcock, who turned out to be the scoring hero of the hour.

Now Everton were in the semi-finals again. Only Trebilcock wasn't there. Neither was Pickering, who had been transferred to Birmingham. Neither was Alan Ball, Everton's £100,000-plus inside-forward, who was under suspension. Fortune, it seemed, might be favouring Leeds United.

But when a goal came, it was scored by Everton. Both teams had defended mightily, and Leeds had had their chances early on. Everton weathered the storm, and came back to score the all-important goal which took them to Wembley. Once more, Leeds United discovered that tears can lie at the end of the rainbow. And it happened again last season, when Leeds lost at home in a replay against Sheffield Wednesday.

But if their dreams of another visit to Wembley in the F.A. Cup final were demolished, at least they can reflect that they *did* reach Wembley in the Football League Cup *... and this time, they came home with the trophy.*

The Football League Cup started off as a competition which many folk in the game said was unwanted. It was just an extra chore which had to be fitted in, at a time when clubs had enough fixture problems, what with League games, the F.A. Cup, European clashes and so on. Not to mention the weather, which could cause a fixture backlog. Leeds didn't look at it that way. Don Revie says: 'I felt that the Football League Cup was yet another opportunity of winning something. It might have started off as a poor relation, but there was only one way it could go, and that was upwards.' His vision proved to be correct, for the League Cup became the passport to Europe.

Leeds started off on the Football League Cup trail with a bye, in season 1960–61. In the second round, they drew, no score, at home to Blackpool, and won the return 3–1. They returned from their fourth-round tie at Chesterfield 4–0 winners, and then travelled down to Southampton, where the fans had their money's-worth in a nine-goal thriller. Unhappily for Leeds, Southampton got the odd goal that mattered.

United reached the fourth round again, the following

IF AT FIRST YOU DON'T SUCCEED... 35

season, when they thrashed Brentford 4-1 at Elland-road, defeated Huddersfield 3-2 in a second-round home tie, and then got a bye through the third round. But in the fourth, they met their match, in the shape of Rotherham, who could only draw 1-1 at Millmoor, but scored two goals to United's one at Elland-road.

In season 1962-63, United again had a first round bye, and in the second round they beat Crystal Palace, 2-1 at Elland-road. However, they came unstuck in round three at Ewood Park, where Blackburn Rovers efficiently disposed of United by a four-goal margin.

Every season, after that, Leeds had a first-round bye. In 1963-64 season, their second-round opponents at Elland-road were Mansfield, who went home licking their wounds after a 5-1 mauling. Swansea were accounted for at Elland-road, 2-0, and then Leeds went to Maine-road, to tackle Manchester City. It was a third-round exit for United, because City beat them, 3-1.

Season 1964-65 saw Aston Villa defeat United, 3-2, in the third round at Elland-road, after Leeds had beaten Huddersfield there by a similar margin. And a year later it was a 4-2 victory over Hartlepools at Leeds, followed by a 4-2 defeat from West Brom, on the same ground.

Season 1966-67 saw Leeds drawn at home to Newcastle, in the second round, and they disposed of the Magpies by the only goal. Then it was a trip to Deepdale, where United had to tackle Proud Preston. The game ended in a 1-1 draw, and the return at Elland-road ended with a comfortable 3-0 victory for United. Leeds, by this time, had acquired a reputation as a team which didn't concede goals often, which was why folk in Soccer were surprised when United went to Upton Park to tackle West Ham, and returned home on the losing end of a seven-goal spree. The wrong United scored all seven, in fact.

Which brings us to season 1967-68—the year Leeds finally made it. For more than 40 years, they had waited to land a major honour in English Soccer. Now, at last, they were to grab their chance, and make up for all the disappointments which had gone before. By this time, too, the Football League Cup had taken on the status which Don Revie had forecast—it had indeed become the passport to a European competition, the Inter-Cities Fairs Cup. Of which, as I said, more later.

A first round bye saw Leeds drawn at home to Luton Town, and they won comfortably, 3-1. Again United were at home, for the third round, when Bury were the visitors. Again, Leeds scored three goals, this time without reply.

Tougher opposition appeared, in the shape of Sunderland, for the fourth-round tie—and this time, Leeds had to travel to Roker. But two goals sank Sunderland, and Stoke City were the next First Division visitors in the queue. Again, United scored twice, without reply from their opponents, and that took them into the semi-finals ... against Derby County.

Derby, managed by former England leader Brian Clough, had won themselves quite a reputation in the competition, and there were those who figured that Clough's crusaders could provide a shock result. But Leeds, who tackled the first leg away from home, kept out the eager Derby forwards, and scored a goal themselves, a comforting thought, as they travelled back to Yorkshire. Derby, however, were not overawed and didn't give up without a fight. They scored twice in the return tie at Ellandroad, but United managed to put three goals past their 'keeper, so into the final they went, to come up against Arsenal.

Like Leeds, the Gunners had had their lean spell—perhaps not quite as long, but certainly just as tedious for their supporters. Under Bertie Mee, however, Arsenal had found a new strength. They had a strong defence, like United, and while they were not noted for scoring many goals, they got the decider which won them the points often enough to suggest that in the near future they would be real challengers for the championship, over 42 hard, slogging games.

And indeed, it proved to be an endurance test at Wembley itself. Two hard, powerful teams, tight in defence, yet with the skill to break away, and everyone knew that one goal could settle the match. So it did, and United scored it. To be precise, left-back Terry Cooper, who had finally won himself a first-team place, after having had spells on the left wing, as well as at left-back.

The critics said it wasn't a Wembley showgame; that hard tackling and defensive play proved an effective deterrent to the forwards of both teams. Well, football is often played that way today, and you have to be skilful exponents of the art of defence and breakaway goals to survive at the top.

The important thing for Leeds, of course, was that this victory registered the breakthrough. For the first time, they were returning from the quest for honours with a gleaming trophy. And, of course, it ensured that they would be in Europe the following season, even if they didn't win the Inter-Cities Fairs Cup, at the second time of asking.

United had reached the final of the European tournament, rated by now as second only to the European Cup, the previous season, and had gone down to Dinamo Zagreb, just as they had reached the F.A. Cup final and gone down to Liverpool at Wembley. But this time, their return from Wembley was as a team of conquerors, with the Football League Cup. And as Billy Bremner, the Leeds and now Scotland skipper observed: 'Now that we've won some silver at last, we'll go on to collect other trophies.'

Billy wasn't a bad judge, either, for the Inter-Cities Fairs Cup was coming up again, with United having reached the final, for the second season in succession. In fact, United, having their third consecutive season in Europe, couldn't have failed to return in the 1968–69 season, even if they hadn't won the League Cup, for, because of their League position, they had qualified for the European competition, anyway. And qualifying *twice* for a tournament must set another kind of record.

Leeds, in fact, had been going for *four* trophies, right from the start of the season. There was the League title, the F.A. Cup, the Football League Cup, and the Inter-Cities Fairs Cup. They failed in that Old Trafford semi-final against Everton, to go out of the F.A. Cup; they faltered at the run-in for the League title, when Stoke City sprang a shock victory over them, admittedly, at the Victoria Ground, as the Potteries club fought desperately themselves for First Division survival; and they finally lost the race for the championship when Liverpool managed to defeat United rather luckily at Elland-road.

So the championship and the F.A. Cup went through the window. But the League Cup went to Leeds, and that left only one more trophy at which to aim—the Fairs Cities Cup. Having tried for four, and seen two honours go by the board, could United travel half-way to success and collect the Fairs Cities Cup, as well as the League Cup? It was an intriguing question, and the answer was close at hand. As we shall see, later in this book. But for the moment, let the players have their say....

3. My debut made me sick

GARY SPRAKE

ONE THING I can say for Leeds United, right at the start—they do give young hopefuls their chance. Today, the accent at many clubs is on youth, as efforts are made to groom home-grown talent and thus save the expenditure of thousands of pounds in the transfer market.

It isn't just that a club saves money, of course, by playing home-produced youngsters; today, there is still an endless search for star players, and big money changes hands, but the ready-made players available are few and far between.

A youth policy is a 'must' for every League club, no matter how humble its status. But Leeds United were in the forefront with a youth policy long before it became so fashionable. And I was one of United's earliest products.

I don't suppose any professional footballer ever forgets the day he made his League debut, and I'm no exception to the rule. Since that day, I've played in hundreds of big games, for my club and for my country. I've played in the team which won the First Division, in an F.A. Cup final, and collected a Football League Cup-winner's medal at Wembley. I've played in European ties, and won an Inter-Cities Fairs Cup medal with Leeds. And I've played against the world's top footballing nations for my country, Wales.

Yet the one memory that still stands out most clearly, and I expect it always will, is of the day I made my bow in the first team. It was a comparatively modest Second Division game, against Southampton at The Dell. And I was a mere stripling of 16.

But that's not the reason I remember this game so vividly. No, there's another reason ... *because it made me sick—and I mean that, literally.*

I had played a few games for the reserve team, and while I dreamed my dreams, of course, I imagined it would be quite a while before my name went up on the first-team sheet. After all, Scotland international Tommy Younger was the regular first-team 'keeper, and it was hardly likely that a young unknown named Gary Sprake would leap into the limelight so swiftly.

My name wasn't on the first-team sheet, either when Leeds set off for that match at Southampton. But a matter of a few hours before the kick-off, Tommy was taken ill, and manager Don Revie, frantically pondering on what to do, in the face of such an unexpected dilemma, made a snap decision. He decided: 'I'll send for Sprake!'

So the message was flashed through to Leeds, on the morning of the match itself: 'Get hold of Gary Sprake, straight away!' And the sting in the tail was this: 'Get cracking and organise an aircraft to fly him down to Southampton!'

When the club officials contacted me, I hadn't even started my breakfast. In fact, with it being match day, even if I were only playing in 'the stiffs', I was still having my Saturday-morning lie-in. But I didn't have time to reflect on matters, for before I knew where I was, I was being whisked away by car to the airport at Ringway, near Manchester.

And when I got there and walked out on the airport 'apron', it suddenly hit me with the force of a thunderbolt. 'There are only *two* people going down—the pilot and myself.' For the plane was no giant Boeing; not even a modest Viscount; it was a tiny two-seater.

Still, it was no time for arguing or anything else. I was wanted at Southampton, and this was the one way of

MY DEBUT MADE ME SICK 41

ensuring that I got there, to make my League debut. By the time I climbed into the aircraft, I don't know which made me the more nervous—the smallness of the plane, or the challenge which playing for the first team offered.

We hadn't been airborne long before I nudged the pilot and indicated that I wasn't feeling too happy, Within seconds, I was confirming that impression, by being airsick. I felt so rough that the exciting visions of football fame rapidly began to vanish. But we were on our way, and the next stop was the airport near Southampton. I just had to grin, well, try to grin, anyway, and bear it.

Manager Don Revie was waiting at the airport, peering anxiously into the sky, as he told me afterwards, for the tiny dot which was to materialise into an aircraft carrying his first-team goalkeeper. As the minutes ticked by, 'the Boss' admitted later, he began to wonder what had happened to the plane. Then, suddenly, we were above the airport and banking for the landing. He gave a sigh of relief, and so did I.

Even then, it was all go-go-go, as our manager hustled me into a waiting car and we sped like mad to The Dell. I was still clutching my football gear, still trying to quell the butterflies in my stomach. Fortunately, by the time we reached Southampton's ground, I had recovered from the airsickness and was beginning to worry about the game.

But there still wasn't time, really, to get into a lather about it, because I had to change in a tremendous hurry, while the referee, linesmen and players of both teams waited. The kick-off had been held up for quarter of an hour, in fact, because of the sudden predicament in which Leeds had found themselves.

As I went on the field, I felt all in a whirl, the sudden summons, the fast drive to Ringway, the sensation of being in another world as we soared aloft in that tiny aircraft, and the feeling that the end of the world was coming, as my stomach started to feel queasy. My mind was a tangle of emotions as I took my place in the Leeds goal, but 10 minutes later, once the action had started, I hadn't time to reflect on the events of the day. I was too busy trying to stop Southampton putting the ball past me.

You might wonder, though, how it happened that Gary Sprake, a real Welsh youngster who had never travelled, became a professional footballer with Leeds United. Well, I'll tell you.

When I was a kid, and I mean a kid, because I'm quite a long way from being 30 now, I lived in Jersey-road, Winchwen, Swansea. Winchwen is just a bit of a village, really, although it had already produced one goalkeeping star in Jack Kelsey, who made his name with Arsenal and Wales. Jack Kelsey, in fact, lived next door but one to us, before he moved to the London club.

I can recall, when I was a toddler, going to watch our local team and, at that time, Jack was a member of it. I don't suppose Jack ever thought that one day I would be following in his footsteps as the goalkeeper of Wales. Certainly I never dreamed such a thing would happen, even in my wildest flights of fancy.

Even when I managed to play football for Swansea schoolboys, I couldn't quite believe that one day I would be an international. Of course, I lived in hopes, but I wasn't really convinced that football fame was around the corner.

However, I followed up by being chosen for my country at schoolboy level, then I picked up youth-international honours. The next step was Welsh Under-23 honours, and by the time I was 20, I was proud to be able to say that I had played for my country half a dozen times in full internationals.

The reason I finished up joining Leeds is simple— United had a scout called Jack Pickard, and he lived in Swansea. As a matter of fact, it was Jack who was responsible for the great John Charles going to Elland-road, and the day came when he asked me if I would travel to Yorkshire and give it a two-week trial period.

MY DEBUT MADE ME SICK

By the end of that fortnight, I had decided I liked the set-up at Leeds and, more important, they had decided that they liked the look of me. So I was happy when they asked me to sign for them as an apprentice professional.

I won my first international cap as an 18-year-old, and it was against Scotland, at Hampden. This honour made me the youngest player ever to appear in goal for any of the home countries. And it was another rush, for I was picked for that Hampden game only a few hours after I had made my Welsh Under-23 debut, against England. When I turned out against Scotland, I was exactly 18 years, 7 months and 17 days old.

Now I'm in my mid-20's, collect pop records and, like many of the Leeds lads, play golf pretty often. And while I'm on about my team-mates, I wouldn't mind if they had *all* been born in Wales! Other goalkeepers tell me, often enough, that I'm lucky to be able to play behind a defence like United's, and I wouldn't argue about that. For my money, there is not another goalkeeper in the League who gets more consistent cover than I do.

4. *Local Boy—from Fulham— makes good*

PAUL REANEY

SOME CLUBS SEEM to overlook local talent. Not Leeds United! True, they have plenty of players on their books who were born many miles from Yorkshire, but believe me, if there is a local lad aiming to make good at Soccer, Leeds United will give him the chance to do just that. I should know.

Now, I was born in Fulham, they have a football club there, too! but as I moved with my parents to Yorkshire when I was only a fortnight old, I reckon I've got the right to call myself a local lad.

And, as a lad, I was usually far too busy playing football to have much time for watching it. In fact, when I signed for Leeds United, in October, 1961, I had seen them play only a couple of times! Up to my joining the Elland-road staff, I had been a footballer in local junior circles. I often played for the school team in a morning, dashed home for a quick snack and a clean-up, then went off to play Soccer for a youth club in the afternoon.

Often, of course, I was whacked by the time I returned home for my tea. But I reckon that even in those days I had plenty of stamina.

Looking back to those days, it doesn't seem any time at all, really, since I was playing for Cross Green School, and yet now I can call myself a full England international! It was a tremendous thrill to be called up for my first cap against Bulgaria last December—a sort of extra Christmas present, in advance. The only pity of it was that my teammate, Terry Cooper, had to miss his first cap through injury.

When I was a lad, playing junior football, Leeds United were far from being the force in top-class Soccer that they are today. They were one of those clubs who hadn't really done anything or won anything, and I suppose some of the older supporters must have been beginning to despair of *ever* being able to cheer Leeds in their moment of triumph.

But since I joined them and graduated through to the first team, things have been great, and not just because I had arrived! It just so happened that my breakthrough came at the same time as United were starting to make a real impact on the game, in Britain and in Europe. And I must say that ever since the day I arrived at Elland-road, I've had nothing but encouragement ... from the manager and his backroom team, from my team-mates, and from the supporters themselves.

In my first season with United, we did pretty well—we finished fifth in the Second Division. That was after a season in which Leeds had given their fans a bit of a fright by seeming to be in danger of relegation to the Third! We followed up that No. 5 placing by coming out of the Second Division the next season—and as champions.

Even better was to follow, for we went surging up the First Division table, and finished the season as runners-up to the champions. Since then, we have known other near-misses—the F.A. Cup final against Liverpool, the Inter-Cities Fairs Cup final against Dinamo Zagreb. But we finally managed to collect two trophies within a very short space of time, when we won the Football League Cup, and then the Inter-Cities Fairs Cup. Now we have made it a treble with the First Division title.

On a more personal note, I've won other honours in the game, too. I made my debut for the England Under-23 team against France in Rouen, and I had a close-season tour which took in Hungary, Turkey and Israel. I played at right-back for Young England against Scotland at Aberdeen, my Leeds team-mate and skipper, Billy Bremner, was playing for the opposition that night! And now I have achieved the ambition every young hopeful aims for, when he sets out on a Soccer career. I have played for the full England side.

As Everton goalkeeper Gordon West, another new cap, said after the England-Bulgaria match at Wembley: 'Whatever happens now, they can't take *this* away from us!'

5. The Day Alan Ball had me 'tickled pink'

TERRY COOPER

WHEN YOU FIND a professional footballer paying an unsolicited tribute to a player of another team, you know he means what he says. And when an England international names a player in an opposing team as 'the best young footballer I've seen this season', then that's a tribute worth having.

When the international's name is Alan Ball, of Everton and England, you know that *he* knows what he's talking about ... and when you read that the 'best young footballer' to whom he is referring is yourself, then that really gives you a feeling of deep satisfaction.

Yes, I was surprised, and tickled pink, when I read that Alan Ball rated me so highly, mid-way through the 1968–69 season, just a few days after we had played Everton at Elland-road ... and beaten them, too. I know Alan Ball is a dedicated professional footballer, through and through; and I know that Leeds United's victory didn't really influence him, in making his assessment. In fact, knowing Alan Ball, that defeat would be the one thing he *didn't* like! For Alan is like me, in this respect—he *hates* to lose.

It's an odd thing, but I have another memory of a game against Everton, too. This time, it was an F.A. Cup-tie at Goodison Park. I didn't play at left-back against Everton, then; I turned out for Leeds on the left wing. And no one was more surprised than I was, because I had gone along just for the ride.

Let me go back to April, 1964, and the start of it all. At that time, I was regarded as a full-back, as I am now, in fact, only in those days I couldn't command a regular first-team place with Leeds. Indeed, so consistent was Willie Bell, who was later transferred to Leicester, that I could get into the team usually only through injury to someone else.

And it was because Albert Johanneson was injured that manager Don Revie sprang the shock news, when Leeds were due to play Swansea Town. This was the game that could clinch promotion from the Second Division for Leeds; a vital game, obviously. And 'the Boss' shook people when he announced that I would be Albert Johanneson's replacement on the left wing, for this match.

Eighteen months earlier, I had been a forward, then 'the boss' had decided to switch me, positionally. Just before that game against Swansea, he brought me into the attack again. I was 19, and although I had tasted the big-time Soccer atmosphere when I played in the second half of a game against Italian club Juventus, this was something different again. For it was my League debut.

I'm a Yorkshire lad, all right, I hail from Pontefract, and I like to think I've got Yorkshire grit. But try as I might to impress, it seemed that I couldn't guarantee myself a regular first-team place in Leeds United's set-up. And they had plenty of other youngsters knocking on the door, so the competition for any position was pretty tough.

Almost a year after my League debut at Swansea, and after plenty more reserve-team games, the F.A. Cup-ties had come round once more. Leeds were drawn away, to Everton. A tough nut to crack, indeed.

I went along in the coach, just for the ride, as I thought. I could have dropped, when 'the Boss' broke the news to me that I would be playing. On the left wing again, and

ALAN BALL HAD ME 'TICKLED PINK'

this time in front of a 65,000 crowd! It was less than an hour before the kick-off that I knew I was in the team, and when we ran out on the field, many of those Everton supporters didn't even know the name of the lad who wore the No. 11 jersey.

It was a bit of a facer, I don't mind admitting, but our skipper at that time, Bobby Collins, saw to it that I soon got over my nerves, and I didn't think I had done too badly when half-time came. But half-time brought with it a change of tactics, too—for Manager Don Revie told me to drop back more into defence in the second half, to mark Everton winger Alex Scott. He was threatening danger all the time, and I must confess I felt a bit more at home defending, too.

However, that still didn't mean I had won a regular first-team spot for myself, and even though I managed to keep making the odd appearance with the seniors, I felt that my progress wasn't fast enough. Even after I had played 20 games in the first team, a couple of seasons or so ago, I still felt that my future chances might be better elsewhere. So I asked to be placed on the transfer list.

It had nothing to do with being unhappy at Leeds—I knew they were a great club, that they had some great players. But ... I was ambitious. I believe you have to be, in this game, and I reckoned that as each season slipped by, my chances of making the top grade must be slipping slightly. Especially with the crop of fine youngsters that Leeds always seemed to be bringing along, and I was no old man, myself, for I was only just turned 20!

Leeds decided, but 'very reluctantly', manager Don Revie told me, that they would not stand in the way, if I were offered the chance of regular first-team football elsewhere. 'The Boss' paid me the tribute of saying that I was 'a great club man', and, with typical shrewdness, talked to me about the future. He told me that, although Leeds were prepared to let me go, he didn't think a transfer would necessarily be the best thing, from my point of view

—in fact, he emphasised that he believed my chances were just as good with United as they would be at any other club.

Well, I thought about it, and I pondered on what 'the Boss' had said. I had asked to go, and had been told that I could leave, if matters developed that way. Yet, deep down, I knew that I didn't really want to leave such a wonderful club, and finally I decided that I would take the manager's advice. I would hang on a bit longer, forget about a transfer in the meantime, and see if I really could make the grade at Elland-road.

For a while, it was still a case of in and out, in and out, then United transferred Willie Bell to Leicester. 'The Boss' sent for me, told me that this was my big chance to establish myself in the first team, and at left-back. I believed in myself, I was determined to take the chance, and it paid off. Now I'm recognised as the regular first-team left-back. And my fortunes have taken a decided turn for the better. In March, 1968, Leeds United were at Wembley for the second time in four years. The first time was when they lost to Liverpool, in the F.A. Cup. The second time was in the League Cup final, against Arsenal, when we won, by the only goal of the game. And guess who scored it—yes, I did! And I was playing at left-back, too.

That goal realised an ambition for myself and my team-mates at Elland-road. For several seasons, Leeds United had fought hard and long to win *something*. Each season it seemed that we were going to collect. But each season something went wrong almost at the last minute. We finished runners-up in the League, we were runners-up in the F.A. Cup. Then we *did* win the League Cup, and we also lifted the Inter-Cities Fairs Cup.

They say that success breeds success. Well, from a personal point of view, I have to agree with this verdict. For along with my regular promotion to a first-team place, I found that my name was being mentioned in connection with representative honours. And I collected an England Under-23 cap. Then came the day, last December, when my name went on Sir Alf Ramsey's team sheet for a full international, against Bulgaria, at Wembley.

Imagine my disappointment, when I received an injury which meant I had to pull out of the England squad. But it's an ill wind which blows no one any good, for my full-back team-mate at Leeds, Paul Reaney, was called up by Sir Alf in my place. As I told Paul at the time: 'Good luck, but I'll be going all-out to get that cap as soon as I'm fit!' And I have not only done that, but I've won a League Championship medal, too.

6. I don't care where 'the Boss' plays me

PAUL MADELEY

WHEN YOU GET the feeling that top-class judges of Soccer potential and talent cannot quite make up their minds if you are going to make the grade, then there's only one thing to do ... try that little bit harder to convince them that you *will* break through. And that's exactly what I did.

I was born within a stone's throw of Elland-road, and so it was natural that I should want to join Leeds United as a budding Soccer professional. At that time, I played for a local club called Farsley Celtic; and I was a lanky youngster.

I won't try to kid anyone, I made a pretty slow start, indeed, I realised before too long that some people thought I was a bit too cumbersome to turn into a really mobile footballer. Today, I'm more than six feet tall, and I weigh close on 13 stone, and I'm still no greyhound. But, thanks to Yorkshire grit and determination, plus the encouragement and patience of those same judges who were admittedly a little doubtful, I have established myself as a member of Leeds' first-team squad.

Everyone at Elland-road has to be prepared to work and fight for his place, and to work and fight for the ball. I've had to work and fight that little bit harder than some of the others, over the course of the past few seasons, and there were times when I really did wonder what sort of job I was going to make of first-class football.

Every time someone was injured or out of the first team, my name would go up on the sheet—full-back, half-back or forward line. By the time I had established myself, I had played in nine different positions for Leeds United, and won the 'Player of the Year' award which is presented annually, when the votes have been counted up, by members of the Leeds United Supporters Club. I was proud of that honour, as proud of it as anything else I have achieved in my footballing career. So right now, I want to say a big 'Thank you' to all those fans who voted for me, at the time.

Now, plenty of people have nick-named me 'Mr Versatile', and I will admit that the tremendous all-round experience I have gained has done nothing but good for me. I even won representative honours, I went along on an F.A. tour of Canada, before I had established myself properly in the first team at Leeds. So willingness to work and play where you are selected, *can* pay off. I'm the living proof of that. Oddly enough, when I did play for that England selection in Canada, I was deputising for our centre-half, Jackie Charlton.

Plenty of people have asked me, from time to time, how I have felt about being the odd-job man, as it were, in the team. It may sound somewhat corny, but it's true, nevertheless. I don't see any reason to make a fuss about such a thing. It's no reason for a player to march in and ask for a transfer; and it's no reason, equally, why a player should feel he requires a larger size in headgear.

The plain fact of the matter is that *any* footballer is a member of the team, and his club is entitled to expect that he plays where he is selected, and does the job to the best of his ability. Which is the line I have always taken. And I know that many of the other lads in the side can play in several positions, and they would be prepared to switch around, too, if it were required of them.

That's the way we have all been brought up at Ellandroad. We're trained to *think*, first and foremost, that we are professional footballers, and that includes doing any team job as well as you know how. Obviously, a professional footballer always lives in hopes of winning honours, at club and representative level. But I've said this before, and I'll say it again: *I don't care where Leeds United play me, just so long as they don't leave me out of the team.*

For that's the most important thing of all.

7. I'm a meek and mild character, really

BILLY BREMNER

'IF FITNESS AND determination count for anything, this will be the season when we get on the honours trail. The Inter-Cities Fairs Cup will do, for a start, then we will get cracking on the issues at home. Every player has trained that little bit harder and, given the run of the ball, we shall not have much longer to wait before giving our fans something to cheer about.'

Those confident words were spoken by Billy Bremner, on the eve of our Inter-Cities Fairs Cup final against Dinamo Zagreb, at Elland-road. When the issue had been decided, the words tasted sort of sour, because once again we had finished as runners-up. League championship, F.A. Cup, Inter-Cities Fairs Cup, Leeds United seemed to be establishing *some* sort of a record, for finishing second-best, in everything. It wasn't the happiest of moments, when we knew that Dinamo Zagreb were the new Fairs Cities Cup holders, instead of Leeds United.

But, at least, the last part of my forecast was bang on the ball. 'We shall not have much longer to wait before giving our fans something to cheer about.'

For, direct from our unsuccessful season in Europe, we returned home to collect the Football League Cup, after beating Arsenal at Wembley, and we went on to become the next holders of the Inter-Cities Fairs Cup. So that, at long last, we all had something to cheer about.

There's a motto in the Leeds United dressing-room which reads: 'Keep fighting.' It hangs above my peg appropriately, for I'm the skipper, and I'm supposed to set an example to the rest of the lads. In fact, every player on the staff knows that motto, and acts accordingly. Leeds do keep on fighting. They never give up until the referee has blown the final cheep on his whistle.

During those seasons of bitter disappointment, we've *had* to keep on fighting, even when we have been down in the dumps. 'The boss,' Don Revie, has walked into the dressing-room many a time, and given us a very necessary pep-talk, after we have tasted defeat in a crucial game like an F.A. Cup final or a Fairs Cities Cup final. And we have emerged from that through a deep depression to vow anew that we *would* win something, some day ... soon. Now we know what it tastes like, to be the champagne victors, instead of the vanquished.

I venture to say that in the past half-dozen seasons or so, we have been one of the most consistent teams in Britain. And I go further—I believe, like Don Revie, that the best of Leeds United is yet to be seen. Our players may be old in experience, but they are young in age, for the most part. And in the next few years, this team with an average age of 25 can be expected only to improve. I think that is a logical assessment of the situation.

They say that I have become indoctrinated with the Leeds brand of Soccer, and that's true. I have been with the club since I left school in my native Stirling, north of the Border, and I have known United in the bad days, as well as the good days. I have also known 'the Boss' ever since he took over at Elland-road, in his first managerial job, and I think along exactly the same lines as he does, when it comes to Soccer planning and tactics.

There is one thing people should remember, too—when Leeds United won promotion from the Second Division, they did it with a team of comparative kids. There were one or two experienced players, like Bobby Collins and Jackie

I'M A MEEK AND MILD CHARACTER, REALLY 57

Charlton, but for the most part, the accent was very much on youth.

Today's championship-winning team has grown up together, played together, and won through together. And I believe that we shall achieve even more together during the coming two seasons for, in my view, footballers reach their peak around the ages of 26 to 27, which we shall do, on average, inside the next couple of seasons.

Having said all that, let me add that I wasn't always a fervent, even fanatical believer in Leeds United. Like Norman Hunter, in fact, I became homesick during my early days at Elland-road, and I wanted to leave and return to my native Scotland. And it took some very persuasive talking by Don Revie before I would agree to give it a real 'go', and allow myself a fair amount of time in which to settle down. I'm glad 'the Boss' talked me out of that mood of depression, just think what I would have missed!

When I lived in Stirling, I played for Gowan Hill Juniors and for St. Modan's High School, Stirling. I was an inside-left in those days, and I won four Scottish schoolboy international caps, which, maybe, was the reason clubs like Arsenal, Cardiff, Chelsea, Glasgow Celtic and Glasgow Rangers were on my trail. But Leeds got to the winning post first, and when I did leave St. Modan's, I crossed the Border and made my way to Elland-road. I'm no giant now, and I was even smaller in those days. I often wonder what the seniors at Leeds thought about the arrival of this little, freckle-faced, flame-haired kid who, so it had been said, could play fooball a bit.

It was 10 years ago last August that I joined Leeds United, and my debut was against one of the clubs that had sought to sign me. I made my first-team bow for Leeds against Chelsea, as a 17-year-old, in January, 1960. I was a stand-in, in fact, for Chris Crowe, and I played on the right wing.

Now, I have hit the headlines often enough since that day, and not always in a manner which I would wish. For

I am blessed (or should it be cursed?) with a temperament which matches my red thatch. Despite my size, I'm a robust player by nature. It's something born and bred in me, and I cannot change it. I doubt if I would, even if it were possible, because then, I feel sure, I would lose the spark which has helped me to make such a success of professional football.

I hate to see an opponent get the ball, and it's my job to see that this doesn't happen, if possible. I go in hard, but fairly, but that temperament I mentioned sometimes erupts, in the heat of the moment. And it's got me into trouble a few times.

Don Revie has had me in his office more than once to talk to me about things. He's given me good advice, told me to try to cool down. It hasn't always been easy to follow this advice, but I've tried and, at last, I really believe I am succeeding in keeping a grip on myself.

I shall never forget when we went to Wembley in the F.A. Cup final. I had landed in trouble with the Soccer powers that be, and I really was afraid that I would be sentenced to a spell of suspension which would put me out of the Wembley showgame. I worried about it, as I travelled on the train to London for the England-Scotland international; I couldn't sleep properly, because of my nagging fears. I'd had four cautions, and I'd got it firmly fixed in my head that I would get a three-week suspension, which would put paid to my hopes of playing at Wembley in the final.

I was with Bobby Collins, who had been recalled by Scotland for that international against England, after having been named the Player of the Year, and Jackie Charlton, who was going to be one of our opponents in that game. Bobby tried to ease my mind by saying that he thought I would finish up by getting just one week and a fine, but that seemed too good to believe. But Bobby turned out to be a good forecaster, that was exactly what did happen. And so I was able to play against Liverpool,

I'M A MEEK AND MILD CHARACTER, REALLY

after all, and finish up on the losers' side!

That was around the time I won my first Scottish cap, it was against Spain, at Hampden, and I said then that I just wanted a Cup-winner's medal to go with it. Now I've three medals since Leeds won the League Cup, the Inter-Cities Fairs Cup and, finally, the League championship; and I have had the honour of skippering Scotland, as well as my club.

I said earlier that I believed I had succeeded in getting that temperament under control, and I have little doubt that the cares of captaincy have had something to do with this. When I say 'cares', perhaps I am using the wrong word, responsibilities is more like it. I take the job of skipper seriously, whether it's for club or country, although I don't let it give me sleepless nights.

But I do realise that, as captain, I should set an example for my team-mates, and so I consciously try to avoid any semblance of trouble or friction, when I'm in action on the field of play. Some folk have suggested that I'm not as 'hard' as I used to be; that I hold back from tackles; that my play has not the same, fiery determination as of old. I don't go along with that. I think the simple answer is that I'm not quite so impetuous, so I don't go rushing in where angels would fear to tread. Certainly not like I used to do. And, therefore I do not run the same risk of ending up in trouble with the referee or my opponent. But in my mind, I have no doubt about one thing—my play has not suffered, and my value to the team has increased.

When it comes to planning, there is nothing any club can teach Leeds United. Manager Don Revie and his backroom staff analyse opposing teams down to the most minute detail, and we go out to play our opponents as thoroughly prepared as possible. This meticulous pre-match planning of tactics makes my job as skipper much easier, I can tell you. Most of the time, our own teamwork and understanding of situations is so good that I can let the lads get on with the job, knowing that they can cope without need of any instructions from me.

I've taken a bit of stick in my time, from opponents and their supporters, but there's one thing I would like to get clear right now. I do not go out looking for trouble. In fact, the way some folk describe me, you would think I was a regular fire-eater. The plain fact is that I set out to do a professional job as a footballer. It's as simple as that.

Off the field, I guess I'm a meek and mild little character, really—I'm human, and I have the same likes and dislikes as anyone else. My favourite foods are bacon-and-egg breakfasts, and salads; I'm a do-it-yourself handyman; I enjoy a round of golf; and I'm a family man who enjoys taking the wife and kids out in the car.

I also make no apology for saying that I'm a Don Revie fan. To my mind, what this fellow has done for Leeds United since he took over as manager is little short of miraculous. And I'm *not* trying to establish some sort of mutual admiration society, when I say this.

In a game where something like 700 managerial jobs have changed hands since the end of the war, you have to have something special to know that your own job is secure. And when you consider that 'the Boss' had had no managerial experience when he was handed the Leeds job, that we were a club really in the doldrums, that he has hauled us from near the foot of the Second Division to the very top of the First, in a few short seasons ... well, I reckon that's a good job well done. Certainly it's no flash-in-the-pan performance. For we have been consistent through and through. And consistency is what finally wins the honours.

8. *I was a one-man awkward Squad*

JACKIE CHARLTON

THERE ARE MILESTONES in every footballer's life. And certainly I can remember quite a few highlights, and low spots, in my own footballing career. The F.A. Cup final at Wembley against Liverpool; our League Cup victory on the same ground against Arsenal; our Inter-Cities Fairs Cup triumph; the World Cup victory which saw England collect the Jules Rimet trophy, after a dramatic victory against West Germany. And now the League title! These are moments in my footballing lifetime I shall never forget.

But in case you think it has been nothing but roses, roses all the way, let me tell you that there was a time, also, when I was a real one-man awkward squad at Leeds United; when 'the Boss', Don Revie, told me: 'If I were a manager, I wouldn't have *you* in *my* team!' Don wasn't the manager then—he was a player, like myself.

Leeds United have been my footballing life, as it were. I'm a one-club man, although I tried hard to get away, at one time! and I can say, in all honesty, that I believe Leeds and Jackie Charlton have been good for each other. I don't think I'm one of the big-headed brigade, but I do believe in telling the truth, and saying what I think. Which is why I'm not wrapping up the bad and presenting only the good things that have happened to me in Soccer.

Life is the same, the world over; it contains good and bad. And it's exactly the same in football: there are times when you're over the moon with delight, times when you feel like crawling away and hiding in a hole. I've heard the Leeds United supporters cheering themselves hoarse for us; I've heard them shouting their unadulterated opinions of us, when things have been going wrong. The paying customer is entitled to voice his view, and the fans at Elland-road are paying customers.

There was a time when I wanted to shake the dust of Elland-road off my feet as quickly as I knew how, and this was probably the lowest point I ever reached in my footballing career. As I said, I'm not the one to wrap anything up, so let's get to the point of this particular story, without further ado.

I joined Leeds United as a 15-year-old, and I'm more than twice that age now, so you can work it out for yourself how long ago it all was. I started as a full-back, made the switch to centre-half, and still didn't get into the first team as often as I would have liked. When I joined Leeds, I felt that they were getting someone who would turn out to be a good player, but as time went on, my mood began to change. My confidence in myself started to fade, and I reached the stage where I felt this club would never make anything—of itself, or of me. In short, I began to feel sorry for myself.

Don Revie arrived at Elland-road as a player who had been around a bit—Hull, Leicester, Manchester City and Sunderland, he had played for all these clubs, as well as England. And, of course, his name had become famous in association with Manchester City's deep-lying centre-forward plan. 'The Revie Plan', they called it. I won't say Don Revie and I didn't hit it off, but we weren't exactly soul-mates.

As a player, in fact, Don didn't hesitate to speak his mind, and quite often I was on the receiving end of his opinions. When things started to go wrong, I used to let it show. And there came a day when Don, bluntly and pointedly told me: 'It would be the best thing that could happen to you, if Leeds left you out, you've got a chip on your shoulder, and you're spoiling it for the other players. You'd never do for me.'

At that time, I had managed to get into the first team, but I was never really confident that Leeds United looked on me as being the man they wanted. You get these ideas in your head, and they grow and grow until you're almost obsessed with such notions. I was obsessed to the point that the only thing I wanted to do was to get away from Leeds United.

Don Revie became the manager, and people like Syd Owen, Les Cocker and Maurice Lindley became part of the backroom team. I saw Syd for the first time, when I went into the office to pick up my wages. Syd came straight to the point, and asked what was wrong between Leeds and myself. I was rude. I told him to 'shove off'.

Instead of getting on his high horse, he just said quietly: 'Give us a chance.' And he asked me to forget about a transfer, at least for a while. He didn't endear himself to me in training, though. I felt he was always getting at me, when he pointed out mistakes I was making. Once, I got so annoyed I was ready to have a stand-up fight with him, and I went to see 'the Boss' to tell him that I wouldn't be responsible for what might happen, if he didn't get Syd 'off my back'.

Well, Syd carried on prompting and shouting, cajoling and criticising, but somehow, I started to forget to feel sore. I found I was actually enjoying the sort of training he and Les Cocker were putting us through. And in what seemed a matter of weeks, I realised I had lost that chip on my shoulder, and was regarding everyone as my mates.

Two or three other incidents stand out in my mind. There was the occasion, soon after he had become manager, and when I was going through my mood of black depression, that Don Revie called me into the office to tell me that he didn't think, after all, that I was the type of centre-half he wanted, and so, if I wanted, I could have a transfer. He also said to me: 'If you played the game right, and did the job you're supposed to do, you would be playing for ENGLAND!' That shook me a bit, and I tried to follow his advice, with good results, as everyone knows.

Then there was the time that the great John Charles returned to Leeds from Italy, and I began to have the nagging thought at the back of my mind that he would finish up playing at centre-half, while I would be out in the cold once more. 'The Boss' must have realised I was suffering from some sort of anxiety complex, because when we were playing golf one day, he took me on one side and, almost as if he were a thought reader, said: 'I'm *not* going to move big John back to centre-half, you know. *You're* there—and you're *staying* there.' That was a load off my mind, I can tell you.

Well, we went on to win promotion, and I became an England international. The World Cup was tremendous, of course, but after it, came the reaction. My play suffered, because I began to get the feeling that after such a fabulous climax, nothing really mattered. I couldn't get myself worked up into any sort of state, before I went out to play in League games. And the day came that the fans started to snipe at me. One gentleman even rang Don Revie one day to say: 'If you don't drop Jackie Charlton, I'll shoot you!'

'The boss' had a chat with me, and persevered with me, and I tried to work up the enthusiasm for the game that I had had of old. And gradually, I found that I was starting to look forward to Saturday again, that things were going right, and that my form was improving.

I once suffered in another direction, too—through injury. I had a ligament injury, and it put me out of the game for several months. Even the medical experts were divided on the best course to take. One felt an operation was the only way to ensure that I played football again, another advised weight exercises and dedication to the task of getting fit again would be the best answer. It was

ABOVE: Peter Lorimer (arms upraised) scores one of United's five goals in the trouncing of West Bromwich Albion at Elland Road in the fourth round of the F.A. Cup in 1967. BELOW: Was it a goal? A lot of United fans thought so when Paul Madeley headed the ball into the net in the third round F.A. Cup game at Hillsborough last season. If it had counted United's lead would have been 2–0, but referee Jim Finney of Hereford (back to camera) disallowed it after consulting a linesman.

ABOVE: Albert Johanneson, *extreme left*, scores the first goal in the third round F.A. Cup replay at Elland Road last season. Sheffield Wednesday, here pictured packing their defence unsuccessfully, hit back to win the game 3–1 and put paid to United's Cup hopes. BELOW: Sheffield Wednesday's Sam Ellis (No. 4) raises his arms in triumph as John Ritchie (not in picture) scores the equaliser just before half-time in the third round F.A. Cup game at Hillsborough last season. Jim McCalliog (No. 8) follows the ball into the net while Peter Eustace (No. 6) looks on. Leeds players are Gary Sprake, Jack Charlton (No. 5) and Mick Bates (No. 10) with hands despairingly on head.

when I was told that 'if you don't play again, there's always a job at Elland-road for you' that the message really struck home. Suddenly, I realised there *was* a serious chance of my playing career being finished.

It took 16 weeks, and extreme patience, as I went through the weight exercises, before I finally could say that the leg was all right, and that I was fit. The muscle wastage had been tremendous, nearly an inch and a half of muscle had disappeared, but by the time I was through, I'd built it all up again. And added another quarter-inch.

By now, I guess you will have come to the conclusion that things haven't always been right between Leeds United and Jackie Charlton, so no one can say that I'm trying to whitewash the club, in any shape or form. Equally, having looked on the black side, no one can deny my right to claim that we have had our good times, our successes.

We went to Wembley, to play Liverpool in the F.A. Cup final a few seasons ago. Maybe you were there. If so, did you feel as I did, after we had lost? Because it seemed to me that day the biggest let-down I had ever known. Not because we lost, but because of the way we lost.

I shall always feel that we didn't do either ourselves or our supporters justice on that Wembley occasion. Maybe because it was our first time there, I felt we needed to justify ourselves. We had started that process of always being runners-up, and never carrying off one of those elusive trophies. I don't know. But whatever the reason, the Cup final seemed a let-down.

In fact, after that game, and while the bitter disappointment still lingered, as we tried to put on a brave face while the champagne flowed at our reception, I made a personal vow. I determined that I would be in a Leeds United team that *did* win something. Again, when we just failed in the Inter-Cities Fairs Cup a few months later, I was choked. But, finally, we made it.

We went back to Wembley, and, although it might not

have been the greatest final that stadium had ever staged, we won the League Cup, when we defeated Arsenal. And we went on to make up for the disappointment against Dinamo Zagreb when we reached, and won, the final of the Inter-Cities Fairs Cup at the second attempt. Then, last season, topping the lot, the League title!

And now for something which has involved Leeds United, and Yours Truly! in plenty of controversy, during the past year or so. This business of Jackie Charlton going up into the goalmouth of the opposing teams, and trying to score goals with his head. It's been termed gamesmanship, obstruction, outright fouling ... and, occasionally, it has been pointed out that it's a legitimate tactic in the art of playing, and winning, football matches.

So let's start at the beginning by saying that some goals come by accident; others are scored by design. And every team in the country practises tactics designed to achieve surprise (and goals) from set positions. By set positions I mean corner kicks, free-kicks, throw-ins and so on. Where the ball is dead, and you have the advantage, because the referee has made the award in your favour.

Leeds United happen to have a team which is prepared to fight hard for the ball, right to the final whistle. They happen to have a manager and a backroom staff who are able to analyse the strengths and weaknesses of opposing teams. The spying missions carried out by people like Syd Owen and Maurice Lindley before we meet our next opponents have proved invaluable, when the game itself has been played.

We also happen to have people who, apart from weighing up the opposition in advance, can plan some tactics of their own, and they see to it that during training, we practise these moves from set positions until they finally work. From such attention to detail has sprung much of our success.

Now, we have a manager who believes that football is a game of physical contact. And we have a bunch of players who are prepared to follow this belief to its ultimate conclusion. That does *not* mean we set out to play it rough; but we *do* intend to get the ball, when we go in for it. If it's an even-money chance, we think we are entitled to go flat-out to win possession of the ball.

Having said all that, let's see what actually happens, when I go up into the opposing team's goalmouth for a Leeds corner kick.

You cannot be offside at a corner kick—so, I stand practically on the line. Now, the trick consists of making sure that you have a player who can kick the ball with complete accuracy and pin-point it so that it is planted right on the head of a team-mate. Indeed, the player taking the corner kick is more important than the fellow standing on the goal line. And we have men like Eddie Gray, Peter Lorimer, Mike O'Grady and Johnny Giles.

They can time and place a pass to perfection, whether the ball is moving or they are taking a kick from a set position. So when Leeds get a corner, and one of them curls that ball over, I know it's going to land right on my napper. All I have to do is make sure that I nod the ball into the net. Simple, isn't it?

No fouls, no obstruction, nothing that is calculated to arouse the ire of any opponent. But, of course, opposing goalkeepers have voiced their disapproval of such a tactic. They have claimed that by standing in front of them, as the kick is being taken, I am impeding them, and preventing them from getting a decent sighting of the ball. They say, too, that when I go up, I am obstructing them from being able to pluck the ball from the air. And, they add, sometimes I back into them which, from their point of view, makes it all the worse.

I say that the referee is the man who decides, and, so far, I cannot recall a referee who has disallowed a goal I have scored in this way. Therefore, the man on the spot has seen nothing illegal about the way I score these goals from corner kicks.

In point of fact, other teams have also used the tactic. Manchester United often send centre-half Bill Foulkes up for a corner kick; Liverpool don't hesitate to make full use of the height and weight of their No. 5, Ron Yeats, in such a situation. And I haven't heard anyone grumble about them. Maybe I've been more successful than most at prodding the ball into the net with my head.

Again, it's up to the opposition to work out moves aimed at preventing me from scoring goals. Opposing 'keepers have done their share of protesting that it's an unfair tactic and so on, but has anyone ever bothered to ask how I get treated in the goalmouth? Sometimes this attempt to score goals results in my going home after the game almost black and blue, from the pummelling I have taken. But I don't remember having cried about the unfairness of it all.

And just to round it all off, let me add that there are times when I don't try to score, even though I go up for corner kicks. I'm acting as the decoy, on such occasions, and we have a signalling system which lets the taker of the corner kick know if I'm wanting the ball sent straight over to me, or if he should place it elsewhere. That has worked on quite a few occasions, I can tell you.

Whenever I go up for a corner, the opposition are keeping a wary eye on me, especially the goalkeeper! They are all expecting the ball to find its way to my head, which means that I can act as a distraction, while another Leeds forward does the scoring damage.

I'm not saying how we work this variation of the corner-kick routine, but I will put one final point. Just in case anyone who reads this should think we're being unfair to goalkeepers and defenders once again, let me say that Leeds are not the only team in which I have played this decoy role.

When England were preparing for the 1966 World Cup, team-manager Sir Alf Ramsey worked out one or two stratagems aimed at fooling the opposition we might encounter along the way. And one of the tactics he employed was to use me as a decoy. I would go up into the attack, when we won a corner, and take perhaps a couple of defenders with me, leaving a gap elsewhere for one of my team-mates to drift in and collect the ball as it came over. It brought us a goal in at least one international match, too.

And I don't remember ever having heard anyone criticise Sir Alf Ramsey and England's World Cup-winning team for employing tactics that could be described as unfair, or savouring of gamesmanship. So why should people get all hot and bothered about Leeds United? As our skipper, Billy Bremner says: If you follow Leeds, and Jackie Charlton scores a goal from a corner, then it's great; if you're on the other side, then it's not the happiest of moments. It all depends whose side you're on.

9. Snap, Crackle and Pop

NORMAN HUNTER

LEEDS UNITED HAVE a tremendous reputation for snapping up young Soccer talent. But when you are an impressionable teenager, you don't always find it so easy to adjust to change, even if your heart is set on making a name for yourself in football. Billy Bremner, for instance, signed for Leeds as a youngster, then wanted to go back to Scotland, because he was homesick. The very same thing happened to me.

I was born at a place called Eighton Banks, and took up football as an amateur with a junior club. My Soccer future was decided, although I certainly didn't realise it at the time, when a Leeds United scout spotted me playing for my local schoolboy team. I was just 15, and it staggered me quite a bit, when I was invited to go to Leeds for a trial.

But that question really made me ponder, before I would commit myself. I realised that I was still only a youngster, and I didn't relish the prospect of leaving home, for I was happy enough where I was. However, Leeds United were a League club, and they certainly gave me the impression that they were about to go places. I was tempted, in the end, and said 'Yes'.

I was still a little uncertain how I would react to moving away from home, when I joined the Elland-road ground staff, but I determined that I would try to settle in and concentrate on football. But, you know, for someone who is still really only a lad, it's difficult to translate words and intentions into deeds.

I can appreciate exactly how the parents of any lad feel, and how the lad himself feels, when a top-class professional football club comes along and makes an attractive offer of a career to the boy. His parents want to do the best they can for him, and they know that Soccer, these days, is a worthwhile career; the lad himself has stars in his eyes, dreams of fame and fortune, of playing for his country and things like that. *But* ... there is almost always the inevitable problem: it means leaving home, if you decide to join the club and carve out a career in Soccer.

You wonder about your team-mates, even at such a junior level. What will they be like? Will they make you feel at home? You feel somewhat overawed by the prospect of suddenly mingling with star players who have been names and faces on the football field, up to then. You have all sorts of doubts and fears. I know, for that was Norman Hunter, when he joined Leeds. And I'll tell you something else. I really did become homesick, in spite of all that Leeds United did, to make me feel one of the family. And make no mistake, they go out of their way to show you that you are part of a family, a great big one, which includes everyone on the staff, from the manager to the humblest apprentice.

But when you're homesick, it's hard for anyone, however kind they may be, to solve this particular problem. There are usually two ways, of course. You persevere, and try to get over the feeling, or you ask for your cards and return home. In my case, there was a third alternative, and it settled the problem in a way which made everyone happy. My mum came to live in Leeds.

But instead of finding that she had just got young Norman back on her hands, she discovered that there were two other growing lads for her to look after, Jimmy Greenhoff and Tommy Henderson, who were both on the books of Leeds United, at that time. It says much for Leeds

United that they realised and appreciated the problems homesickness can bring.

I had made a couple of pals, meantime, goalkeeper Gary Sprake and right-back Paul Reaney, who were making their way through the Leeds United Soccer 'academy', like myself. We were virtually inseparable—Billy Bremner used to call us 'Snap, Crackle and Pop!'

And when I found that I was back 'home' I really began to settle down and concentrate on the business of becoming a professional footballer. I was 19, when I made my first-team debut, which is another thing that goes to prove Leeds United will give you your chance, no matter what your age. By the time I was 20, I had established myself as a first-team regular at wing-half, and I had collected an England Under-23 cap. Today, I'm happy and proud to say, I have played for England at full international level.

When I look around the dressing-room, and see the lads who joined Leeds as mere youngsters, like myself, I realise more and more that we have been lucky. Lucky to have had the chance to play for Leeds, and win international and representative honours, in the process.

Gary Sprake, of Wales and Leeds; Paul Reaney, of England and Leeds; Terry Cooper, of England and Leeds; Billy Bremner, captain of Scotland and Leeds; Jackie Charlton, of England and Leeds; myself; Johnny Giles, of the Republic of Ireland and Leeds! Mick Jones, of England and Leeds; Eddie Gray, of Scotland and Leeds; and Mike O'Grady, of England and Leeds.

Oh, yes, I'm forgetting, Mr. Versatile himself, Paul Madeley, who can play at full-back, half-back or in the forward line. A couple of seasons or so ago, Paul went on an F.A. tour of Canada. I went, too—and I can tell you that I thought Paul was outstanding. Sir Alf Ramsey, who was the team manager, was really impressed, too.

Plenty of managers have been on to Leeds, during the past few seasons, to ask if the club were prepared to part with Paul. Those inquiries were regular occurrences, during the days that Paul was standing in for players who happened to be out through injury. Nowadays, of course, Paul is an established first-teamer himself. And it's no wonder that 'the Boss', Don Revie, firmly told all interested parties who inquired about the chances of signing Paul: 'Sorry, but he's not for sale, not even at £200,000.'

Paul, like myself and all the other lads at Leeds United, typifies the family spirit which has been built up. We are part of the team, and we play for the team. What's more, we play as a team. And that sort of spirit is something that *no* money can buy.

Norman Hunter

10. He's United's No. 1 Supporter

NOW LET'S TAKE a break from the Soccer stars themselves ... and give a spot to one of the people who help the club in another way. 'They also serve, who stand and wait' ... that's how the saying goes. Well, Leeds United fans waited long enough for their chance to cheer. And here is the story of one of them....

Arthur Dunhill just missed being elected Britain's No. 1 Soccer fan a few months ago, he came fourth in the voting, but there is no doubt that he must rank as Leeds United's No. 1 supporter. After all, Arthur has seen Leeds play close on 500 games in the last nine years, and that includes matches abroad, as well as home and away in this country.

Arthur is a true football fan. He says: 'I try to be fair in my assessment of a game. Of course, I love to see Leeds United win, but only if they deserve to do so.' Indeed, he looks back over all the games in which he has watched Leeds play, and singles out *another* United as the team which topped the lot. That was West Ham United.

Arthur says: 'West Ham defeated Leeds 7-0 in a League Cup-tie a few seasons ago, and the football in that match was really superb.'

Arthur is a bachelor; he is in his early 50's; and he runs a newsagent's business at Bramley. It allows him time to follow football all over Britain, and he has forked out as much as £400 in his Soccer travels during the course of a season.

Arthur doesn't confine his watching to the First Division games, either. He has seen Leeds play in F.A. Cup-ties, Inter-Cities Fairs Cup matches, League Cup-ties, friendly games, Central League matches, and even West Riding Cup games.

And while he is an avid Leeds United supporter, he has watched more than 300 other matches during the past three years. All of which takes up most of the leisure hours of this genial follower of football.

Many a time, indeed, Arthur Dunhill has travelled to an away game, arrived back in Bramley around four o'clock in the morning, got straight down to the job of sorting out the papers for the day, snatched three or four hours' sleep before lunch, and then set out to watch yet another match that evening!

Facts and figures can be boring, but they can also be enlightening. And the staggering, overall fact is that Arthur Dunhill has covered more than 200,000 miles in his pursuit of Soccer. What's more, he hasn't got a car! He makes a careful study of the fixture lists, the weather forecasts and the railway timetables, and works out how to get where he's going. He has never been off course, either ... and has been late for the kick-off on only three occasions. Some going!

This was the third successive season in which he has seen all 92 League clubs in action, and his log book is a real mine of information about distances he has travelled and games he has seen. For instance, he watched 157 matches and travelled 27,175 miles in season 1966–67; 185 games and 31,463 miles in season 1967–68. And he was travelling around again, last season.

Yet Arthur will admit, without being pressed, that there will be many Leeds United supporters who have seen their favourites more times than he has. There is a simple explanation for this, although it is somewhat surprising, too.

For Arthur, who was watching Leeds United long before

the war, was running a junior team for Leeds Wanderers in the local Red Triangle League, right up to the time he began to follow Leeds around, week by week. And he set a high standard in his association with the local club, because in 25 years, he missed only two of their matches!

And just in case you think that he has jumped on the bandwagon of success—forget it! Arthur Dunhill was following Leeds United when they were struggling near the foot of the Second Division. In fact, he can recall making the long haul to Plymouth and back, when he was the *only* Leeds supporter to make the trip.

Today he says: 'The days when United were struggling have vanished—and for good. Manager Don Revie and his players deserve tremendous credit for the terrific job they have done. And the great thing is that Don and his backroom team have built up a situation where the future of the club is assured for many years to come. Most of the first team are still young, and good for several seasons' service, and there are other youngsters, plenty of 'em, who are ready and waiting for their first-team chance.'

We salute Arthur, and we hope he will be following Leeds United around, home and away (abroad, too, for that matter) for many more years to come.

11. *High Drama in Europe*

LEEDS UNITED'S EXCURSION into Europe began in season 1965–66. Almost immediately, they were involved in high drama, coupled with an element of tragedy. Bobby Collins, their pocket general, the human dynamo who had been such an inspiration in United's climb from Second Division obscurity to the lofty reaches of Division 1, was brought to earth with a crash, and there he lay, his leg broken. It happened in Turin.

United, making their first essay into European competition, had started their quest for Fairs Cities Cup glory by tackling Torino at home, and had come out of that encounter with a 2–1 lead. Leeds went to Italy knowing that so long as they kept a clean sheet, they were through to the next round and, as their defence marshalled itself magnificently in the first 45 minutes, so their hopes rose. Indeed, at half-time, United felt that they could afford to venture in search of another goal, and sew the whole thing up.

But five minutes after the resumption of play, disaster struck. Bobby Collins was going hell for leather for goal, when Torino full-back Poletti went racing into the tackle. Collins fell to the ground, and that was the end of him, in this game.

Jackie Charlton says: 'As soon as I saw Poletti going in, and watched Bobby go down, I knew the "wee man" had broken a leg. Our trainer, Les Cocker, spent five minutes trying to assess the damage, and see if he could get Bobby back on his feet. But it was no use. A thigh bone was broken, and I could have cried when they carried Bobby off, muffled in Don Revie's raincoat. All at once, instead of going for that "killer" goal, we had to start thinking defensively, again.'

Leeds shuffled the pack: they had only Peter Lorimer and Alan Peacock as strikers upfield, while Torino swept down upon the United defence time and again. But as the final moments ticked away, the score was still 0–0, and so Leeds lived to fight again, although they had to travel back without skipper Collins, who lay in the Maria Vittoria hospital, awaiting an operation which, happily, proved a success.

Even today, Don Revie views this display by his team as one of their greatest ever. 'They all worked like Trojans, to make up for having lost Bobby,' he says. 'And the way they tackled the job proved beyond all doubt what tremendous professionals they were.'

As for Bobby, he underwent a 60-minute operation, after which the doctors announced that he would be able to play again. And play he did, although it meant months of grinding, slogging work before he regained full fitness.

From Italy, it was on to East Germany for Leeds, who had been drawn against Leipzig in the second round. And when it was all over, United marched on, again by a 2–1 aggregate. Which meant that they faced Valencia, of Spain. And again, there was high drama in the match at Elland-road. It ended in a 1–1 draw, but before the final whistle had gone, both teams were down to 10 men.

Valencia scored first, and that left Leeds with a desperate fight to pull out an equaliser, so that they might stand at least a chance in the return game. At last, Leeds did score, and then they threw everything in, as they sought a winner. With barely a quarter of an hour to go, the game erupted, as Jackie Charlton went up into the attack, and found himself being kicked and punched.

Jackie says: 'I admit I lost my temper, suddenly, I was conscious only that I had been singled out for some diabolical treatment. They said I went berserk. All I know was that I wasn't going to take any more of this, without giving some of it back. Even my own team-mates could not restrain me, I was so angry.'

All at once, it seemed, players were going at one another, as tempers flared. Police appeared on the field, and Dutch referee Leo Horn walked off with his linesmen, signalling to officials of the two clubs that they should get their players into the dressing-rooms. The unofficial interval lasted 11 minutes—11 minutes in which the players could cool off, and start to think about football again. When they returned to finish the game, Jackie Charlton and Valencia left-back Bidagany were not with them. They had been given marching orders.

Even then, the excitement wasn't over, for with little more than five minutes to go to the end of the game, Valencia inside-forward Sanchez-Lage was sent off, too, after having kicked Jim Storrie.

Of course, there was intense speculation about what would happen in Valencia, when the return tie was played. The war of words went on and on, but when the return game did take place, a fortnight later, it proved to be a complete triumph for Leeds. And those who had gloomily predicted a bloodbath were made to eat their words.

This time, referee Horn was not in charge of the game; instead, a referee and linesmen from Switzerland were named to handle the match. And Leeds United confounded the critics who had written them out of Europe by scoring the only goal of the game. Paul Madeley started the move which brought the goal. He pumped a 30-yard pass right over the full-back's head, and Mike O'Grady collected the ball, raced on with it, and sent the ball whizzing past the Valencia goalkeeper, who had moved out to try to narrow the angle. So Leeds United, on their first tilt at Europe, were in the quarter-finals, and there they saw off the Hungarian team, Ujpest Dozsa, on a 5–2 aggregate. Which put United into the semi-finals, and up against Real

Zaragoza, the Spanish team whose forwards were named 'The Magnificent Five'. And they had not acquired this reputation for nothing. Zaragoza's attack was something for opponents to admire—and fear. As Leeds finally acknowledged.

The first leg of the semi-final was played in Zaragoza, and Leeds hit trouble again, for they were subjected to some fierce tackling, body-checking, and outright fouling. Johnny Giles, for instance, was grabbed by the neck from behind, then struck in the kidneys, on one occasion very early in the game. He ended up receiving marching orders, in fact, with fewer than five minutes to go. But as anyone who has seen Johnny play will readily agree, he is one of the game's cleanest players, which says quite a bit for the treatment which United's opponents had been dishing out.

Zaragoza's forward line tried all they knew to crack United's defence, but it seemed that the 'Magnificent Five' were destined to go goal-less, for once, until, during a real bombardment of the Leeds goal in the second half, they won a corner. Marcelino, the leader of the attack, managed to outjump Norman Hunter and nod the ball past the clutching hands of Gary Sprake. Billy Bremner, standing on the line blocked the ball with his arm, and referee Marcel Bois pointed to the penalty spot. Lapetra squeezed the ball home, although Gary Sprake made a magnificent effort to save the spot-kick.

The second leg of the tie was at Elland-road, one week later, and inside half an hour, United had wiped out that one-goal lead of Zaragoza's, when Jackie Charlton went up into the attack and pumped the ball past the Spanish goalkeeper. But in the second half, Zaragoza came back to score again, which meant they were ahead once more, on aggregate.

Leeds switched Jackie Charlton to centre-forward, in a desperate endeavour to level the scores again, and within three minutes, United were back in the hunt, for they

ABOVE: Don Revie and Bertie Mee, the Arsenal manager, lead out their teams for their League Cup final battle at Wembley. BELOW, *left*: Skipper Billy Bremner introduces The Boss, Don Revie, to Princess Alexandra before the League Cup final with Arsenal at Wembley. BELOW, *right*: Billy Bremner holds the Football League Cup high on the steps of the Leeds Civic Hall after the home-coming reception. Congratulating him are the Lord Mayor and Lady Mayoress of Leeds, Colonel and Mrs. Lawrence Turnbull.

ABOVE: The goal which brought Leeds United their first major honour. Terry Cooper, *extreme left*, slams the ball through a packed Arsenal defence at Wembley to bring the Football League Cup back to Elland Road. BELOW *left to right*: The late Albert Morris (former chairman), Terry Cooper, who scored the winning goal, skipper Billy Bremner and manager Don Revie pictured with the Football League Cup after United had beaten Arsenal 1–0 at Wembley.

ABOVE: Here you can see why Leeds United don't concede many goals. Packing the defence as an opponent shoots are Jack Charlton (No. 5) and Gary Sprake with Billy Bremner (No. 4) and Paul Reaney on the goal-line – just in case. BELOW: Penalty king, Johnny Giles, sends West Ham goalkeeper Bobby Ferguson the wrong way with a spot kick at Elland Road. Looks dead easy, doesn't it?

ABOVE: FA Cup second replay against Sunderland at Boothferry Park, Hull. United won 2–1 after drawing 1–1 at both Roker Park and Elland Road. Rod Belfitt scores one of United's goals. BELOW: The final whistle has gone and Rod Belfitt has given his lot. Trainer-coach Les Cocker has to give him treatment for cramp before he can get off the field into that well-deserved bath.

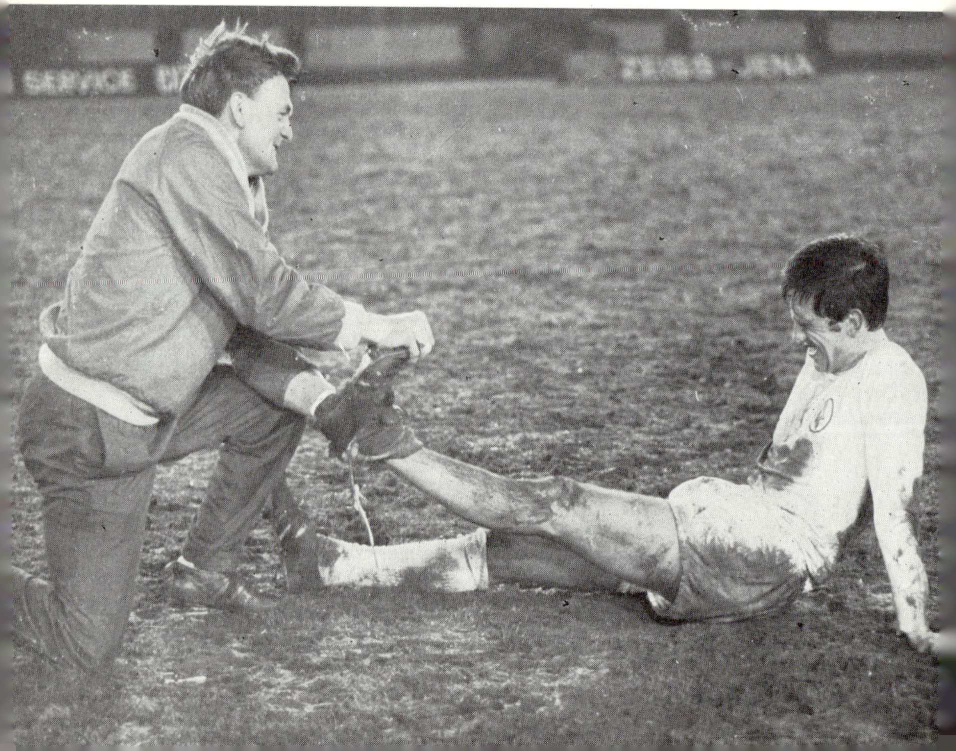

scored once more, to lead 2-1 in that game, and be level on aggregate. Norman Hunter was the man who put the ball across for Jackie to nod it beyond the reach of goalkeeper Giocoechea. And that was how the game ended—a 2-2 draw—and the replay venue to be decided by the flip of a red-and-blue disc.

Officials of both clubs gathered in the centre circle, where Jackie Charlton and Lapetra stood, as the referee flipped the disc into the air. The 45,000 fans went silent, as the disc spun, and Jackie Charlton called 'Blue'. As the disc hit the ground, Jackie, white-faced, couldn't bear to look; he turned his head away, then Don Revie's excited cry of 'You've done it!' rang through his ears. The Leeds skipper had indeed called correctly. United would stage the semi-final, sudden-death play-off.

And that set another problem, for England had an international against Yugoslavia scheduled within 24 hours of the play-off game, and Sir Alf Ramsey wanted Jackie Charlton and Norman Hunter. United's trouble was worse still, because Paul Madeley, who would normally have stepped in for big Jack, was out of action with cartilage trouble. Leeds asked for a new play-off date, and the Fairs Cup organising committee agreed that the game could go on on May 11, instead of May 3. But Zaragoza started to pose problems, then.

A telegram arrived at Elland-road from the Spanish club. It said that Zaragoza had already arranged a charter flight for the game on May 3. And it seemed that, come what may, the Spaniards were intent on playing the game on that date. It was even suggested that they might claim victory by default, if United didn't turn out on that date, but in the end, the May 11 date stood, and so the stage was set for another titanic battle.

It was the night Leeds lost out, despite having ground advantage and the support of thousands of their fans. 'The Magnificent Five' really came good: they scored a goal after play had been going for one minute, which meant that United were fighting for survival virtually from the kick-off. In fact, inside 13 minutes, United were down—and out of the Inter-Cities Fairs Cup.

Villa stabbed a pass across the face of goal for the lurking, dangerous Marcelino to flick the ball into the net. That was goal No. 1. Violeta pushed the ball through the middle, and Villa slammed home a fantastic left-foot drive. Goal No. 2. And still only five minutes of the game gone, when Santos whipped in a shot from ouside the penalty area, Gary Sprake was deceived by the flight of the ball, and that counted for goal No. 3. The United fans were silent as the grave. Finally, in the second half, Leeds did manage a goal, by Jackie Charlton. But it didn't make any difference to the result, and so United were out of the final, which had been so near.

That, then, was the end, the unhappy end, of their first venture into European football. United were not disgraced, but it was just one more bitter disappointment to add to the list of near-misses which they had been chalking up with monotonous regularity.

However, once more there was consolation to be gained from the knowledge that they would be back in the Fairs Cities Cup tournament the following season. United had a first-round bye, and accounted for D.W.S. Amsterdam by an aggregate score of 8–2, to reach round three which, it seemed, was where they came in. For their opponents were none other than Valencia, the team who had been involved in such a furore the previous season.

United scored after six minutes, in the Elland-road first leg, but the Spaniards regained the initiative and equalised. Jimmy Greenhoff scored United's goal, Claramunt netted for Valencia, and everyone said: 'Well, that's it—Leeds can say good-bye to Europe for another season, at least.' Manager Don Revie admitted: 'I was hoping we would go to Spain for the return with a two-goal lead. Now it means we have a lot of hard work, in that game. But it isn't all over, yet.'

About 75,000 people packed the Mestalla Stadium in Valencia for the return, and it seemed as if 74,900 of them were cheering the home team. But by the end, they had been reduced to silence. Leeds defended valiantly, sometimes desperately, as the Spanish forwards bore down upon goal and sought to pierce the United defensive barrier. But they couldn't score, while United scored *two*.

Some of United's established first-teamers had been unable to travel, through injury; young Terry Hibitt was playing his first senior game; and when Leeds scored their second goal, they were down to 10 men. Under such circumstances, the only word to describe their performance was: 'Magnificent.' And it was a term thoroughly deserved.

It was a night to remember—for Leeds, and for that genial little Irishman, Johnny Giles. Only minutes before he ran out on the field, Johnny had been handed a telegram which told him that his wife has given birth to a little girl, and how Johnny celebrated. Inside 10 minutes, he had shocked the crowd of Spanish supporters by scoring a goal for Leeds. He was half-way in the Valencia half, as he collected a pass from Peter Lorimer, and cut diagonally across the pitch, while Peter and Rod Belfitt acted as decoys, drawing the Spanish defenders the other way. Johnny's shot, low down, left goalkeeper Pesudo gaping in amazement.

Valencia threw the lot at United, but they couldn't get through. And they had their chances, despite the tremendous defence by the Leeds lads. Indeed, Brazilian inside-right Waldo, the top marksman in the Spanish League, squandered several chances of levelling the scores ... On one occasion, he had nothing to do but put the ball in the net, yet he managed to fire it wide. However, as they say in Spanish ... Esto es Futbol. That's football ...

Valencia were desperate to equalise, and they were anything but gentle in their tackling. In fact, when Leeds got their second goal, Eddie Gray was over the touchline, having attention to a cut eye. There were but three minutes to go, then, when Paul Madeley shot for goal—only to see the ball beaten out. Johnny Giles swooped on it, passed it across to Peter Lorimer, and the young Scot rammed it home from close range. And then it was all over, with Leeds through to the fourth round, against Italian team Bologna. It was a game which, after both legs, saw the score remaining at 1–1. Again, a flip of a disc was required to settle matters—this time, to determine which team should go through to the semi-finals. And again Leeds called correctly.

For the second time in the Inter-Cities Fairs Cup tournament, their luck was in. But even so, manager Don Revie echoes the sentiments of another top British manager, Liverpool's Bill Shankly, when he says: 'Flipping a disc is farcical, in a competition of such importance.'

Don believes that the only way to decide a winner is to play the game out to a conclusion, but he also accepts that extra fixtures are time-consuming, and that these days, time is something which can ill be spared.

So he adds: 'At least, the winners should feel that they have progressed because of some measure of superiority over their opponents, such as scoring from penalty kicks. Three penalties could be taken at each end, say, with six different players taking the spot-kicks.

'You could even play 15 minutes' extra time each way, with each side minus a goalkeeper and two other players, for the first quarter of an hour, then six-a-side for the final quarter. True enough, your first reaction, when you realise you have won the call as the disc is spun, is one of thankfulness that you are through, but you soon realise how the opposition must be feeling, when they know they are out. And you begin to think, "There, but for the grace of God...".'

It was Leeds who were lucky against Bologna, though, and they went into the semi-finals against Scottish team Kilmarnock, whose hopes took a rude shattering when Leeds emerged the overall winners by four goals to two.

And so into the final, against Dinamo Zagreb, of Yugoslavia. A final which ended with Leeds doomed to yet one more disappointment, as Dinamo showed pace and punch enough to win the trophy, by scoring two goals without reply. The goals came from two breakaways, during the away leg, and Leeds could not get through the Dinamo defence in the Elland-road return. But they were there again, in the 1967-68 season.

This time, they broke new ground by playing Luxembourg team C.A. Spora, and they had a record 16-0 triumph. The second round saw United drawn against Partizan, Belgrade—the team which foiled Manchester United in their European Cup quest a few seasons ago. What Manchester United failed to do, Leeds achieved. They defeated Partizan on a 3-2 aggregate, and so they came up against Hibernian, one of the two Edinburgh teams. A 2-1 aggregate saw United march into round four, which saw them up against another Scottish club, Glasgow Rangers. The two games against Rangers attracted a fantastic amount of interest, so much so that closed-circuit television was brought into action, to enable all the fans who wanted to see the ties to do so. The game in Glasgow was piped live on T.V. at Elland-road, and the return fixture was seen on closed-circuit T.V. by thousands of Rangers fans who swarmed to Ibrox. The first leg was at Ibrox, and Leeds United succeeded in their quest. They went with the avowed intention of getting a draw, and they returned knowing that they would start level on their own ground.

United never gave Rangers a chance of snatching back the initiative when the Elland-road return was played. Leeds scored twice, to go through to the semi-finals for the third year in succession.

And for the third game in succession, United came up against Scottish rivals. Having disposed of Hibernian and Rangers, they took on Dundee, who were all out to avenge the defeats of their compatriots, and, at the same time, get through to the final themselves. But once more Scottish schemes 'ganged agley'. When the two ties had been played, it was Leeds United who were the overall winners, by a 2–1 aggregate. Exit Dundee... enter Ferencvaros.

12. Final Triumph in Budapest

For once, the disappointment came first; to be followed by the moment of triumph which Leeds manager Don Revie and his players, not to mention the United supporters, savoured to the utmost. The disappointment? That was the result of the first leg of the Inter-Cities Fairs Cup final against the Hungarian team, Ferencvaros.

After 90 gruelling minutes, during which United lost two key forwards and had to field two substitutes, the scoreline showed Leeds to be one solitary goal ahead. Not enough, most of the critics argued, to win the Fairs Cup, considering that the return game would go on in Budapest. But, then, that's the sort of situation which is made for Leeds United.

Manager Revie summed it up succinctly: 'It will be tough, but we have faced this sort of thing before. We kept a clean sheet, and if we score over there, Ferencvaros have to get three.'

The first leg was played at Elland-road on the night of Wednesday, August 7, 1968, just a few days before the English First Division campaign. Fewer than 26,000 people went through the turnstiles ... largely because the date was bang in the middle of the Leeds holidays, and the match was also televised for the whole 90 minutes. So the disappointment came early, from the point of view of support. The thrills didn't exactly come fast and furiously, either.

This was Leeds United's line-up, at the start: Sprake, Reaney, Cooper, Bremner, Charlton, Hunter, Lorimer, Madeley, Jones, Giles, Gray.

Before the game was over, the referee had awarded 45 free-kicks, 24 of them against Ferencvaros, and Rod Belfitt had substituted for Mick Jones, while Jimmy Greenhoff had come on to replace Johnny Giles. Giles went off after 65 minutes—he was concussed; and soon afterwards, Jones left the field with a groin injury. But before his departure, he had scored the goal which at least put Leeds in with a chance of final victory. It wasn't much but, as events turned out, it proved to be enough to win the Inter-Cities Fairs Cup.

Ferencvaros, not unexpectedly, had decided to play it hard and defensively. They strung out a front-line screen of three men; and they soon brought centre-forward Florian Albert back to slot into the defensive scheme of things. So Leeds United were battering away at a team which put the accent on defence in depth.

Even so, there was one nightmare moment for the Hungarians, when goalkeeper Geczi was awarded a free-kick almost on the line, and he miscued the ball straight to Jones, who was lurking near the edge of the penalty area. Jones swiftly slotted the ball in Lorimer's path, and he shot hard, only to see Geczi make amends for that free-kick with a dazzling save, which brought Leeds a corner.

But United could not profit, nor did they fare better from two more corner kicks.

And it was Ferencvaros who had the chance to make the running, for a time, after that. Indeed, the United defence was caught on one foot, as Fenyvesi sprinted down the wing, then crossed the ball to Szoke, bang in front of goal. But by the time he had tried to make sure, it was too late. Instead of a first-time shot, he switched the ball from left foot to right. And the chance was gone.

Leeds began to send up their half-back reinforcements, and Charlton and Bremner backed up Jones in challenging for the ball, almost under the Ferencvaros bar. And with about five minutes to go to the interval, it was Jones who won a corner kick.

Lorimer swung the ball across; Charlton, in his familiar position of being virtually on the goal line, won the ball in the air, and nodded it down to Jones, who forced it into the net. So United went in one goal up, and hoping for more in the next 45 minutes. They were doomed to disappointment.

Indeed, they were given a real fright when Albert, forsaking his defensive role, raced away and split the Leeds defence with a pass which Szoke took in his stride. This time Szoke did shoot—but wildly. He could have given Albert the return, and brought about a real panic in the United reargard. But once more, Szoke made the wrong decision.

Giles went off mid-way through the second half, suffering from double vision, and Greenhoff replaced him; Ferencvaros took off Fenyvesi, and substituted Balint. With five more minutes gone, Belfitt was replacing Jones, who had clashed with the Hungarian goalkeeper. Jones was in full stride, going for a long ball, and Geczi raced from his line in an attempt to intercept. Both players went down, inside the penalty area, but while Geczi got to his feet quickly enough, Jones lay inert, and was finally carried from the field.

Both teams missed chances of scoring soon afterwards—first Leeds might have doubled their tally, when Greenhoff shot weakly from inside the six-yard box, and then Rakosi failed to beat Sprake, with a wide-open goal at which to aim. Sprake leaped to his left, and brilliantly took the ball sideways in the air.

There were no more chances going begging for either team, and so the stage was set for a thriller in the Budapest return. Today, manager Don Revie still recalls the feelings of doubt he had, when he considered United's chances in the return encounter. 'I knew that we had faced up to such situations before, and emerged the victors,' he says. 'But this was the final, the moment of truth—and I wondered, for one thing, if the law of averages would work for or against us. I did not admit the doubts I had, of course, and I tried everything I knew to inject confidence into the Leeds players. But, privately, I was more than a little worried about the outcome of the second game.'

Ferencvaros were rated the finest team in Europe, at that time, and although they had concentrated on a spoiling game, overall, at Elland-road, Revie knew that centre-forward Albert, for instance, was likely to be a much more dangerous proposition playing an attacking role in the Budapest match. Indeed, Ferencvaros were going to throw the lot at Leeds, as they sought first an equaliser, then a knock-out winner.

The Hungarian inside-men, Varga and Rakosi, had shown some dazzling footwork and inter-passing in the Elland-road game, and they would be going flat-out to punch holes in the United defence in the second encounter. The accent would be very much on attack, in that game.

Leeds would have been in a much stronger position had a scoring effort from Billy Bremner counted. Indeed, Bremner still insists that his header was handled by Novak, as it was about to cross the line.

But if Ferencvaros were in attacking mood in Budapest, they soon came to realise that two can play at defence. For, just as Ferencvaros had been virtually unyielding at Elland-road, so were Leeds United rock-like and immovable in Budapest. They defied all the efforts of the Hungarians to break through, and they walked off the ground in the knowledge that they were, at last, winners of a European trophy.

It might not have been entrancing to watch, as a defensive exhibition, especially for the Hungarian supporters; but it was a fascinating display of how to contain your opponents who are hell-bent on scoring goals against you. And no one played a greater part in containing the Hungarians than Terry Cooper, Paul Madeley and Norman Hunter. These three were unbeatable.

Ferencvaros persisted in trying to force their way through down the middle of the field; and that was where they were consistently bottled up. If it wasn't Hunter, Madeley or Cooper stopping them, it was Jack Charlton, heading the ball away from danger. And when they did get through, occasionally, they found Sprake in brilliant form.

In Florian Albert and Varga, Ferencvaros had two players who constituted a real menace to United. They schemed and wove their way into the Leeds half with the ball, they grafted and they sprayed passes around with fluency. But all to no avail. The 75,000 crowd packing the Nep Stadium quickly sensed what the pattern of the game was going to be—all-out attack by Ferencvaros, and a stubborn rearguard action by Leeds United.

Twenty minutes had passed before the first real moment of danger threatened Leeds, but when it came, it was a close call. United, as usual, were packing their penalty area, as Ferencvaros mounted another assault, and it hardly seemed possible for anyone to get the ball through, but Rakosi thought otherwise. He jinked his way within shooting range, and let fly, leaving United defenders with their hearts in their mouths. Then, from nowhere, it was Terry Cooper who took the eye, and cleared the danger. One moment the ball was travelling goalward, the next it was curling through the air in the opposite direction, as Cooper plunged in and took an all-or-nothing overhead kick. And within a few more minutes he had come to the rescue again, when Albert sent a fierce low shot.

For 35 minutes, Ferencvaros kept up the pressure, and United defended stubbornly, brilliantly, and at times a trifle luckily. But they do say that fortune favours the brave, and there was not a man among the Leeds defence who wasn't prepared to risk all, in the bid to foil the Hungarians.

People were beginning to look at their watches and think about half-time, which was but a few minutes away, when Leeds themselves broke away and gave Ferencvaros a fright. They won a free-kick, which was taken by O'Grady, and Jones leaped skyward to launch a header. His luck was out for, although he got to the ball, it hit the crossbar. But this lone attack gave Leeds encouragement, and twice soon afterwards they went close to scoring goals, but were defied at the last gasp by goalkeeper Geczi.

The final moments before half-time saw the traffic once again flowing towards the United goal, but the whistle went without any score having been signalled, and United grabbed thankfully at the respite which gave them a chance to take a breather.

United knew that with only 45 minutes remaining, and the score still 1–0 in their favour, they could expect a renewed bombardment as soon as the game restarted. Manager Don Revie says: 'During the interval, I thought fast and furiously, as I talked to the lads. I was grateful that we had survived the first half without conceding a goal, and proud of the Leeds players for the way they had withstood the Ferencvaros attacks. I couldn't help but tell them how well they had done but, at the same time, I knew I had to warn them against becoming over-confident. Those first few minutes of the second half, when we might tend to be relaxed initially, could lead to disaster for us. I tried to hammer it home that the moment play resumed, it would be another 45 minutes of sheer, slogging endeavour.' And how right Revie was.

Immediately the referee's whistle signalled the restart, Ferencvaros made tracks for United's goal. Right-winger Szoke raced down and hammered in a shot from the wing which could so easily have been missed by a less brilliant goalkeeper than Sprake. But the Welshman flung himself across goal and clutched the ball safely.

Within a few minutes, Ferencvaros had set up another attacking move, which almost brought a goal, when the

FINAL TRIUMPH IN BUDAPEST

ball was suddenly and unexpectedly back-passed, and gave another Hungarian attacker an opening to shoot. But he drove the ball wide, and so United escaped again.

Then it was Varga wafting over a curling centre, and Rakosi getting to the ball and trying a first-timer ... only to see it go wide. And so the pattern of play continued, with United marshalling their defensive forces expertly and calmly, taking everything that their opponents could throw at them.

Now time was on United's side, and running out for the Hungarians. There were but 15 more minutes to go, and everyone sensed that the drama was being played to its close. Ferencvaros had taken off Szoke, and replaced him with Kraba; and Leeds had brought on Bates for left-winger Terry Hibbitt. Mick Bates found that he wasn't required as an attacker, though, for with the minutes ticking slowly by, everyone on the United side was pulled back into all-out, massed defence.

Ferencvaros had a couple of moments of hope, when Varga tried an overhead kick into the centre, but the bounce of the ball beat his own team-mates, as well as the Leeds defence. That was let-off No. 1. The other came when centre-forward Albert collected the ball, and hared for goal in a breakaway move which left United defenders trailing and looking on helplessly, as Sprake came out to meet the threat. Courageously, Sprake dived at Albert's feet, and smothered the danger. And that was just about that. When the whistle sounded for the end of the final, it was still Leeds United 1, Ferencvaros 0. And so Leeds had added the Inter-Cities Fairs Cup to the Football League Cup they had won at Wembley the previous March, by beating Arsenal by the only goal of that final. United, in fact, had created a bit of footballing history, too, for they had become the first British team to capture the Fairs Cities Cup. They ranked alongside Manchester United, Tottenham and West Ham as European trophy winners.

The road to Budapest and final triumph had been hard and long. It had been littered with disappointments in this and other competitions. There had been near-misses twice in the First Division title race; failure in the F.A. Cup final against Liverpool at Wembley; and failure in the final the previous season, against Dinamo Zagreb.

United's travels, in their successful safari, had taken them through Luxembourg—they defeated Spora 9–0 away, and 7–0 in the Elland-road return; through Yugoslavia—they beat Partizan Belgrade 2–1 away, drew the return 1–1; through Scotland, three times—they beat Hibernian 1–0 at Leeds, drew 1–1 in the away encounter, drew 0–0 against Glasgow Rangers at Ibrox, and defeated them 2–0 in Leeds, drew 1–1 away to Dundee, won 1–0 at Elland-road; and finally, through Hungary.

In those games, more than 178,000 people saw them play at Elland-road, and millions more watched United on television. Eleven players shared the goals which United put past their opponents. The scoring went like this: Lorimer four (one penalty), Greenhoff two, Bremner, Madeley, Jones—all against Spora in Luxembourg; Johanneson three, Greenhoff two, Cooper, Lorimer—in the Elland-road return.

Lorimer and Belfitt in the 2–1 victory against Partizan in Belgrade, and Lorimer again in the Elland-road 1–1 draw;

Gray in the Elland-road victory over Hibernian, and Charlton in the Easter-road return;

Lorimer and Giles (penalty) in the game at Leeds against Rangers;

Madeley in the 1–1 draw at Dundee, and Gray in the winning 1–0 return;

Jones in the first leg of the final against Ferencvaros at Leeds.

By general consent, the final in Budapest was one of the most exciting scoreless draws ever seen, and the trophy was presented to skipper Billy Bremner by Sir Stanley

Rous, president of the Fairs Cup committee. It was, perhaps, fitting that it should be a Scot who received the cup from an Englishman, for Leeds United had become the first British club to win this tournament, in the 10 years of the competition in which games were played as far apart as Norway and Italy, Northern Ireland and Asia Minor.

One of the best features about the final, too, was that despite the tremendous pressures on both teams, the fouls were not noteworthy nor too often. The game was played under the watchful eyes of the top brass of Soccer from many European countries, and when it was all over, there were many compliments paid to both teams about the way the players kept their heads and their tempers.

The game that brought a European trophy to Leeds was played on Wednesday, September 11, 1968. Exactly a week later, Leeds United, the holders, began their defence of this crowd with a game in Belgium against Standard Liege. And Ferencvaros, the defeated Fairs Cup finalists, set off on yet another European mission ... this time, involving the European Cup. For they had finished as champions of the Hungarian League, and so qualified to meet Levski Sofia, of Bulgaria, in the first round of the European Cup. People like Sir Matt Busby, of Manchester United, and Jock Stein, manager of Glasgow Celtic, rated Ferencvaros as just about the best side in Europe, which made Leeds United's glittering conquest all the more memorable.

13. The Luckiest Day in my Life

MICK O'GRADY

WITH A NAME like O'Grady, I should be an Irishman, which I am not. But I am the fifth son of an Irishman, in fact. But although my Dad came from County Mayo, he crossed the Irish Sea to England, married a Yorkshire lass, and settled in Leeds. That's where I was born, and as a Soccer-playing schoolboy, I played for Leeds City and Yorkshire Boys. So why, then, did I not join Leeds United right at the start?

Sure, it was touch and go whether I joined United when I left school and chose to make professional Soccer a career. But, somehow, I felt that my future looked rosier if I settled for Huddersfield, and so, instead of Elland-road, I went to Leeds-road. Even then, it wasn't a racing certainty that I would be purely a footballer, for I had ideas about qualifying as a draughtsman, as well, and for a spell I continued my studies while I was learning my Soccer trade with Huddersfield.

But fame can come swiftly in football, as I found. And when it does, many of your preconceived notions go hurtling out of the window. So when, after 10 League games, I was awarded my first England Under-23 cap, I decided to forget about a desk job. I was 18, and I had places to go, Soccer-wise. By the time I was 20, I had collected a full

ABOVE: Leeds United footballers travel thousands of miles by air every season to meet commitments in Britain and Europe. They are here seen boarding a plane for yet another trip. *From top to bottom* they are: Reaney, Hibbitt, Giles, Cooper, Bates, Charlton, Jones, O'Grady, Lorimer, Harvey, Madeley, Hunter, Greenhoff (now with Birmingham) and Sprake. BELOW: Mick O'Grady gets the winner against Manchester United in last season's League game at Elland Road. Also in the picture besides goal-keeper Alex Stepney are Old Trafford players Stephen James, Nobby Stiles, Tony Dunne and Pat Crerand.

ABOVE: Recognise the ground? If it was not for the crowd on the right it could be any junior arena. It is, of course, Elland Road under reconstruction. BELOW: Don Revie and general manager, Keith Archer (second from right in back row) with the backroom staff who keep the wheels turning on the administrative side. Groundsman Ray Hardy, whose staff did such magnificent work in the big freeze in February, is on the extreme right.

England international cap. Then came trouble, in the shape of a back injury.

Injury is a vocational hazard so far as professional footballers are concerned, of course. Every day, the Soccer-going public reads about this player or that player being out of action with a pulled muscle, a knee injury and so on. Occasionally, you read that a player has broken a leg or an arm or a collarbone, and that he will be out for several months. But you always think it happens to the other fellow—never to you.

Well, it happened to me. For a long time, I was troubled by that back injury. Just when I seemed to have got over it, I would feel a twinge again, and I was in and out of the game for a lengthy spell. That sort of thing doesn't do your confidence any good, and you even start to wonder if the finish of your footballing career is looming up. When you are just turned 20, such a prospect is too awful to contemplate but, as I said, it doesn't exactly encourage you to sparkle. I know there were occasions when I 'nursed' the injury, even while I was playing; it may be that subconsciously I was afraid of something going. However, in the end, I overcame any hesitancy I might have had about going flat out for the ball in a 50–50 race for possession against an opponent. Only the trouble was that by that time I had become unsettled at Huddersfield.

My old boss at Leeds-road, Bill Shankly, had moved on to Anfield, and he was starting the build-up which took Liverpool to so many honours. But when he tried to sign me from Huddersfield, his luck was out. I thought mine was, too, especially when I read that he had finally signed Peter Thompson from Preston.

Finally, Huddersfield did agree to let me have my wish, and I was told that I could go, which was where Leeds United, my home-town club, stepped in. And now I believe that it was the luckiest day in my life that Leeds gave me a second chance to join them—not that I didn't have my problems when I moved to Elland-road. Injury struck again, and for quite a while I could never count on being a regular member of the first team. This was no fault of Leeds, right enough, but again I began to wonder if I were fated to be one of those unlucky players who never really gets started.

Again, there were times when I was out of action for lengthy spells, times when people must have wondered: 'Whatever happened to Mike O'Grady?' I can tell you that there is nothing so grinding as a fight back to fitness and form. They talk about the loneliness of the long-distance runner, but a footballer striving to regain fitness is equally lonely. Not because his team-mates shun him, or because the training staff ignore him; but because he must do so much of the work on his own. While others can play together and against each other in a five-a-side, for instance, the man battling to regain fitness will be lapping on his own round the track, or doing special remedial exercises in the gym. It's a hard slog, even when you are constantly encouraged to keep at it. But the only thing to do is to grit your teeth, persevere, and tell yourself that one day soon, all the effort will have been worth it. I told myself that a million times, and I'm thankful to say that the effort *was* worthwhile, in the end.

Although I might add that there was a time when Leeds were prepared to let me go. They had paid Huddersfield around £30,000 for my services; and when Northampton offered them a £5,000 profit, they decided to give me the choice—I could stay, or I could join Northampton. I turned down the chance of that transfer and I have never regretted it.

Now I am back in the first-team set-up, I have (I hope) got over that injury jinx, and I believe that I am playing as well as at any time in my career. I have learned a tremendous lot about the professional approach to football since I arrived at Elland-road, and with that knowledge, and a return to full fitness, has come confidence, increasing with every game. And to cap it all, I won back a place in the England squad last season.

14. The Lessons I learned at Leeds

JOHNNY GILES

I AM ONE of the few players who arrived at Elland-road via another top-class club. So I have a very good yardstick by which to measure the quality and the potential of Leeds United. Most of the lads in Leeds' first team are home-produced. They were signed as youngsters and groomed through the various junior sides until they achieved first-team status. And, bearing in mind my knowledge of that other Soccer 'academy', Manchester United, I can say that there are still plenty of talented youngsters coming through at Leeds, lads who will be knocking on the first-team door before very long. In my view, the future of Leeds United as a top-class footballing power is secure for years to come.

I am now in my sixth season with Leeds, and I can honestly say that I have never regretted making the move from Old Trafford. Manchester United were famed, way back, for their policy of spotting young talent, signing such lads, and grooming them through to first-team places. I was one of the players who joined the 'academy', and I can tell you that the standard was high, the competition fierce. It doesn't seem so long ago that almost every lad who had Soccer stars in his eyes would tell you, when asked which club he would like to join: 'Manchester United.' It seemed Old Trafford had almost a monopoly, when it came to snapping up star material.

THE LESSONS I LEARNED AT LEEDS

I arrived at Old Trafford as a starry-eyed lad from the Emerald Isle—from Dublin and the Stella Maris junior club there, to be precise. I was a comparative nipper of 15, and it was quite a thing, I assure you, to go down for training and meet the established first-teamers who had a string of international caps between them.

Another little fella, Nobby Stiles, was a contemporary of mine; in fact, Nobby and I became great pals, and he ended up by marrying my sister, Kay. Side by side, Nobby and I fought our way into the first-team reckoning at Old Trafford but, as I said, the competition was fierce. We were in, we were out ... and we were in again. I was luckier than Nobby in one respect. When Manchester United went to Wembley in the F.A. Cup final, Nobby was ruled out through injury, but I played, and went up to receive a winner's medal. But after the Charity Shield game against Everton, at the start of the following season, David Herd, Albert Quixall and myself were axed. So I decided that, for me, this was the Soccer crossroads. It was August, 1963.

Now, it took a lot of pondering on my part, before I finally decided that I wanted to leave Old Trafford. I had been there right from the start; I had made many friends in Manchester; and I had played plenty of First Division football in my time at Old Trafford. But, somehow, I felt as if I were the office boy. Let me hasten to add that no one at Old Trafford ever suggested this was so, but I felt it. I had joined them as 'a little lad' and, in spite of being happy there for most of the time, in spite of the glamour of going to Wembley, I was still conscious of being 'a little lad'.

Maybe it was some sort of an inferiority complex, I just can't pin it down, even now. But I do know that I could never convince myself that I would ever rank alongside the great names who had been, and still were, on United's books. So ... I asked for a transfer. Results came more quickly than I had expected.

Within 48 hours, Leeds United had talked to United,

and Leeds manager Don Revie was telling me what a great future lay ahead for me with *his* United. Again, I pondered, but, in the end, I felt that I might as well make the clean break from Old Trafford, and that Leeds would be as good a club as any to join. I admit I didn't quite share Don Revie's enthusiasm, at that time, for the future prospects of Leeds. I thought they had some potential, but I honestly doubted if they were going to be as good as Don promised me.

I didn't tell him, of course! Privately, I had decided that they were not quite so big as Manchester United, that I was likely to feel much more at home at Leeds, even if they didn't get among the real honours of the game. So I signed, and I made my debut in a home game against Bury. I didn't really know much about Leeds, even then—I'd played against them, but only in the reserves.

I heard later that within 24 hours of my having joined Leeds, they could have made a handsome profit on my transfer, by selling me to Manchester City. I don't know if it's true but, in any case, I'm glad it never came to the point. After all, Leeds hadn't really had any time to see if I measured up to the fee they had paid for me, in any case.

When I joined Leeds, of course, Bobby Collins, another 'wee man', was very much the king-pin of the attack. Bobby had arrived from Everton, and played a tremendous part in Leeds' run of success. At Old Trafford, I had played at inside-forward and on the wing; at Leeds, I realised that Bobby was the key inside-man, the general of the attack, and so I found myself playing on the right wing. I preferred inside-forward, but I was quite prepared to do my best in whatever position Leeds decided to play me. Eventually, of course, after Bobby left for Bury, I moved inside, and I'm now recognised as the schemer myself.

Now, whenever a player leaves one club for another, there is always one game he awaits with more anticipation than any other, and that's the match against his old team. Since I joined Leeds, of course, I've played against Manchester United pretty often, and I still get an extra kick out of knowing they are our next opponents. But the game that sticks in my mind, above all, is the one in which we met them at Nottingham Forest's City ground. For it was an F.A. Cup semi-final, in 1965.

In the first place, the semi-final went on at Hillsborough, and the teams drew. So the replay went to Nottingham, and what a dramatic climax it turned out to be. There was nothing between the teams with only a couple of minutes to go, to the final whistle. It seemed that the deadlock would still not be broken, that extra time was the one hope of sorting things out. Then Leeds were awarded a free-kick. I was deputed to take it, and it landed just right for Billy Bremner to head the ball into Manchester United's net. I hadn't scored the goal, but I had laid it on, and I can tell you that it meant a tremendous lot to me, although I could sympathise with Nobby Stiles in his disappointment.

In fact, it was a night for cheers and tears all round, because Jackie Charlton had just learned that he had won his first England cap, for the game against Scotland at Hampden, and he and brother Bobby, who sat with Nobby Stiles in the losers' dressing-room at Nottingham, would be teaming up for their country. It was a pity that when we met Liverpool in the final at Wembley, we had to finish up as losers. But you can't win 'em all....

When I left Old Trafford, I had already collected 11 caps for the Republic of Ireland, and since I have been at Elland-road, there have been quite a few more come my way. So I lost nothing, internationally speaking, from my move to Elland-road. But I really do feel I gained a tremendous amount, too.

I was always confident in my ability to play skilful football. I knew I could beat a man, I knew I could pass the ball accurately. But Leeds taught me something else—that *work* and *will to win* are just as vital as any instinctive skills you may possess. Manchester United had plenty of big names, plenty of stars; Leeds had still to build their name, their reputation. So, although there were plenty of players with ability, they all had to be prepared to do any kind of job on the field, for the good of the team all round. It didn't matter who you were, you had to 'muck in', as they say in Yorkshire. If there were weaknesses, you had to be prepared to graft and cover, and you knew that every other player in the team was prepared to do exactly the same, if you made a mistake yourself, or ran into trouble. And that, I am convinced, is the basic secret of the success we have achieved.

15. *Goals are My Business*

MICK JONES

GOALS ARE MY business—that's why Leeds United paid £100,000 to Sheffield United for my transfer. I must admit that there are times when business in my department has not seemed so brisk, but I must also say that I really believe there is an explanation which deserves to be given. So here goes....

Every scoring forward misses more chances than he would like to miss; and I'm no exception. I have scored some pretty vital goals for Leeds, and I've missed a few sitters. But the fact remains that scoring goals is one of the hardest tricks of the trade in Soccer, and there are quite a few tricks, believe you me.

Most teams visit Elland-road with but one thought uppermost in their minds—to avoid defeat. They certainly don't set out with the intention of winning a match, away at Leeds. That's the sort of reputation United have, throughout Britain and on the Continent. 'It's almost asking the impossible to give 'em a licking ... so set your stall out to make sure you don't lose.' The result is that Leeds United have to break through what is virtually a human wall, to get a sight of their opponents' goal. Not surprisingly, under those conditions, goals are not so easy to come by.

As I said, most teams visit Elland-road with their target set in advance. They're out to get a draw. And in the face of such a defensive set-up, the front men in the Leeds attack come in for some tight marking. I'm the front runner of the front runners, and I accept that I must take plenty of weight, plenty of stick in the job of trying to score goals and, at the same time, open the route for others.

You've heard it said it doesn't matter how you score 'em—just so long as you score 'em. That's true enough. It doesn't really matter, either, who scores 'em—just so long as the goals are coming. Well, goals never come as often as a team would like, but we have developed quite a system for sharing out the prizes. In fact, every member of the team, apart from the obvious exception of goalkeeper Gary Sprake, counts himself a potential scorer of goals.

Go through the list, and you'll see what I mean. Left-back Terry Cooper won us the League Cup with his goal; Jack Charlton has earned us many a valuable point with his napper, when he goes up for corner kicks. Paul Madeley, Billy Bremner, Norman Hunter, Johnny Giles, Peter Lorimer, Eddie Gray—the long, the short and the tall ... they all know how to find the net, given the chance.

Yet I must admit that goals are what give me a kick. I've dreamed of scoring goals for as long as I can remember, and that goes back to the day I scored *fourteen* in a Cup semi-final for Priory Secondary School in Worksop. We actually got sixteen, but the other two didn't belong to me. We could have given them to our opponents, though —for they didn't manage a solitary one!

When I scored those 14 goals, I made up my mind that it would be Soccer for me. I was chosen for Worksop Boys, and then on three or four occasions I played for Nottingham Boys. When I left school, I joined Dinnington Miners' Welfare as an inside-forward, and started work as an assembler in a local cycle factory. So if anyone remembers buying a bike with the wheels on wrong way round, you can probably blame Mick Jones!

Yes, my mind was rarely on my work, I must admit. I

dreamed about Soccer ... about scoring the winning goal in an F.A. Cup final at Wembley. And then, after 10 months with Dinnington, Sheffield United began to show a flicker of interest in my displays as a footballer.

I was invited down to Bramall-lane to train as an amateur, a couple of nights a week. And I was chosen for a couple of games in the junior side. I couldn't have done so badly, either, for after a month I was given the chance to go on the ground staff. I jumped at it.

In those days, before the Blades' spending spree, after they had raked in £200,000 for myself and Alan Birchenall, Sheffield United relied almost entirely on home-produced talent. And they still have plenty there, I can assure you. They brought up their youngsters through the junior sides, and you can take it from me, this is the way to foster a great club spirit. It's the backbone of any club, and I've seen how well the system has done for Leeds United.

I must confess that I didn't collect any youth honours, but I did collect plenty of stuff which the departing fans had left on the terraces. I spent quite some time, during a period of 18 months or so, sweeping the stands and cleaning the boots of idols like Joe Shaw and Cec Coldwell. And after those 18 months were up, I was given the chance to turn full-time professional.

Within six months, four days before my 18th birthday, to be precise, I made my League debut. Against Manchester United, at Old Trafford. On my birthday itself, I played against Manchester City, at Maine-road. So that must constitute some sort of a double. What's more, I scored two goals in that game against City.

My first League goal will stick in my mind as long as I live. Wing-half Brian Richardson sent the ball over, as I raced through the defence. City goalkeeper Harry Dowd came out, and I collected the ball and lobbed it over his head, and into the net. I've scored a few more since that day, knocking on for a century of goals, in fact, in League and Cup.

That first goal, at Maine-road, is one memory; another is the goal I scored in the first leg of the Fairs Cities Cup final against Ferencvaros, at Elland-road. Jack Charlton went up for a corner, and was standing practically right on the goal line. The ball came over, I suddenly found it had been pushed out to me, so I promptly stuck it into the net. And, as we drew 0–0 in the return game, I suppose I can claim my goal won the Inter-Cities Fairs Cup for Leeds.

However, as I admitted earlier, I've missed plenty of chances. I'm still wondering how I managed to fail with two openings in the third-round Cup replay against Sheffield Wednesday last season. I was only a few yards out from their goal, and it pains me when I think that if I'd snapped up the chances, we would have had at least the chance of a second replay. As it was, Wednesday won 3–1.

I said I didn't win youth honours at Bramall-lane, but I did manage to collect England Under-23 honours. The first was against Rumania, at Coventry, and I scored our first goal, in a 5–1 victory. Then, in 1965, I collected two full international caps, against Sweden and West Germany, when Sir Alf Ramsey was sorting out his World Cup squad.

I can tell you now that I never got the wanderlust, or felt that Sheffield United were an unfashionable club. I believed that if I were good enough for honours, I would win them with The Blades. Indeed, I was quite content to spend the rest of my footballing career at Bramall-lane. Lots of stories go the rounds about footballers, from time to time; I know many folk said that I had demanded a transfer from Sheffield United. But it just wasn't true.

Leeds United came along for me, however, and I felt that this was an opportunity I could not afford to turn down. I have never regretted my decision to make the short move across Yorkshire, either. I was sad to leave 'The Lane', but I'm in this game for a living, and the cash involved and the chance to join a top club like Leeds was too good to miss. It didn't worry me, either, that Leeds had paid

United a staggering £100,000 for my transfer. After all, I didn't set the price on my head.

Leeds manager Don Revie put me at my ease straight away, for one thing. He said, simply: 'Forget all about the cash—go out on the field and enjoy yourself. Do your best, and that's the way you will repay us.' I've always tried to do exactly that, since I arrived at Elland-road.

In fact, the only grouse I've got about having joined Leeds United is that somehow, the lads won't let me win a 'house' when we have our pre-match Bingo sessions! It just seems as if everyone can win, but me. The moment I'm ready to shout, someone pips me on the post.

If I'm happy at Leeds, and I am, it is only right that I should pay a tribute to someone who did a tremendous lot for me at Bramall-lane. John Harris. They tell me he was a hard man, when he played at full-back for Chelsea. And I don't doubt that was true. Well, he certainly taught me that Soccer is a *man's* game, that you have to be ready to give and take the knocks. And it was he who first stressed the value of team spirit. It's a lesson I hope I shall never forget.

Believe me, I've found that professional football is a lot harder than assembling bikes, but it's worth it! The rewards for success have been far beyond my wildest dreams, I will candidly admit. The greatest thrill to date has been that Fairs Cities Cup triumph, when we walked off the park in Budapest knowing we had won the trophy. But there are a few other highlights in my footballing life.

Believe it or not, but my favourite ground is Hillsborough ... yes, despite that F.A. Cup knock-out last season from Sheffield Wednesday. After all, we did draw on their ground, first. In fact, I've played at Hillsborough seven or eight times, and I've never yet finished up on the losing side, with either Sheffield United or Leeds United.

My biggest disappointment was when we lost to Everton in the F.A. Cup semi-final at Old Trafford last year. It's every footballer's ambition to play in a Wembley final, and I was choked to think how near I had come to making it. So near... and yet so far.

If we're going to talk about players, then I'll say now that the best centre-half I've ever come up against is big Mike England, of the Spurs. He's strong and commanding in the air, determined in the tackle, and amazingly skilful on the ground, for such a big fellow. If they were all like him, I reckon I would pack it in as a centre-forward, and have a go in defence!

Now my next ambition is to help Leeds into the European Cup, and if I can make 'em, never mind score 'em, on the way there, I'll be happy. It's a funny thought, really, but I've never yet managed a hat-trick in top-class football, despite those 14 goals I once scored in a much lower grade. So perhaps a hat-trick in Europe would be another thing to dream about.

And just to round it off, here's another odd reflection. My Dad was a goalkeeper with Worksop Town. He spent his career trying to keep 'em out ... I'm spending mine trying to bang 'em in the net. Here's hoping...

16. *Never Mind my Dad,
Leeds are 'tops'*

EDDIE GRAY

I'M NOT THE first Scot to have landed on his Soccer feet, after having been born in Glasgow, in an area not far from the Gorbals. And I don't suppose I'll be the last to cross the Border in search of Soccer fame and fortune.

Since I arrived at Elland-road, some very nice things have been said about the way I play football. There have been critical voices raised, too, at times, I admit. But the point I want to make here is that whatever has been said about my ability (and I'm referring to the good, now), I'll never be in danger of being big-headed. You see, whenever I go back home, I have to face my uncles, and *they* insist that I'm nowhere near as good a player as my Dad was. They also tell me I never will be!

I owe a tremendous lot to my Dad, in any case. He played at wing-half with Greyfriars, a Glasgow junior team, before the war. It was the war that finished his career, for he was wounded, and that put paid to his Soccer-playing days. So he had to settle for watching, and the team he chose to support was Glasgow Celtic. He used to take me along with him, and it was always understood, in fact, that if ever I turned out to be a good enough player, that would be the club for me. Celtic were the greatest club in the world, so far as my Dad was concerned, and I don't think he's forgiven me yet, for having thrown in my lot with Leeds United. If you don't believe me, just ask him—it nearly broke his heart when I didn't join his beloved Celtic.

So I suppose I'd better tell you now how it all came about. Well, I played for Glasgow Boys, and then for Scotland Schoolboys against England, Ireland and Wales —and I *did* get an offer from Celtic. But I was also given the chance to go down to Leeds, and have a look round the Elland-road set-up during my Christmas holidays. Frankly, I believed I was going down south on what would turn out to be merely a token visit—I never really expected to get caught up in the Leeds United fervour.

But, somehow, when I did get to Elland-road, I couldn't help but be impressed by the way everyone treated me. It was that wonderful family spirit which you will read about so many times in this book. It may be repetitive, but, honestly, I couldn't get away from the fact that there *was* something special about Leeds. All right, so I was still a starry-eyed schoolboy, but the spell was cast, so far as I was concerned. I just felt at home. I simply decided that, Glasgow Celtic or not, Elland-road was the place I wanted to be, and I have never been disappointed since that first day.

Now, in those early days, there was a thing I couldn't settle, and that was the digs. Jimmy Lumsden, a pal of mine from Glasgow, and a wing-half on the fringe of the first team now at Leeds, moved six or seven times before we finally agreed: 'This is it. These are the digs for us.' And it was another Scot to whom both Jimmy and myself owe a great deal, wee Bobby Collins, then starring with Leeds, was especially helpful with advice and encouragement, during my days as an amateur.

I signed full-time professional for Leeds when I was 17, and made my League debut against Sheffield Wednesday at Elland-road. I don't know if any Leeds fan will recall the occasion, but I remember I scored, although, frankly, neither goals nor games stand out for me, really. I go on the field to try my best and play as hard as I can for the 90 minutes; and the moment I walk off, I know it's the next match that counts.

One game I could not forget, though, was when I was chosen to play for the Scotland youth team—and I cried off. Because I had also been named in the Leeds United team which was playing away against Real Zaragoza, in the Inter-Cities Fairs Cup. It was my first taste of European Soccer.

However, I was chosen by Scotland later, for the Under-23 game against Wales at Wrexham, and then against England, at Newcastle. And I played for the first (but not the last, I hope!) time at Wembley when Leeds won the Football League Cup against Arsenal. In fact, that's the game I remember best, I should think, mainly because it was one of those days when I couldn't do a thing right. To be blunt, I had a stinker.

I've mentioned Bobby Collins as having been helpful to me, when I was a raw kid, not that I'm any age now, really, but, I couldn't pass up this chance without a few words about Syd Owen and Les Cocker, too. They have taught me a great deal about this exacting game, and one of the things about them which impressed me was their patience, when I wasn't able to play for almost a season, after I had injured a thigh muscle playing for the reserves against Sheffield Wednesday at Hillsborough. I was only 16 then, and it was a long, slow job getting fit again.

I'll admit it now—there were times when I thought I was washed up. Times when I felt that the slogging grind of trying to regain fitness would only end up in failure. But all the time, Syd and Les kept going at me. Between them, they often worked four stints a day on getting me back into good physical shape, and they refused to allow me to think that it might be a waste of time. Whenever they sensed that I was becoming downhearted about the battle for fitness, they made made the extra effort to cheer me up. I'll tell you something else, too—they were hard taskmasters. But if it hadn't been for them and 'the Boss', Don Revie, I really believe I would have given up the ghost and turned my back upon football.

One more confession, and then I've finished. I don't particularly like playing with the No. 11 on my back, for I prefer to have a midfield role. But, like Paul Madeley, I'm ready to play anywhere in the team, just so long as I *am* in the team. I know I've still a lot to learn about the game; but I know, too, that I have the right men around to teach me. To me, Leeds United are the greatest club in the world—and never mind what my Dad says about Celtic!

17. The Night 'the Boss' was caught Speeding

PETER LORIMER

I CAN CLAIM to have set one record, in my comparatively short career so far as a professional footballer. I became the youngest player ever to appear in Leeds United's first team in their League history. And, at the time, I made my bow against Southampton, Leeds had been a League club for 42 years. I was 15, and the date was September, 1962.

I had had eight outings with the reserve side, at centre-forward and inside-right, but when I was plunged into League football proper, because of the injury situation at Elland-road, I wore the No. 7 jersey. As a schoolboy footballer, I had earned something of a reputation as a scorer, by the end of the 1961–62 season, I had slammed home 176 goals, and there were quite a few clubs who had expressed interest in me. But Leeds won the chase for my signature, and I've never regretted making Elland-road my choice.

I was born in Angus, and played for the Scottish schoolboy international team. By December, 1963, I was coming up to my 17th birthday, and celebrated by being chosen for Scotland F.A. amateur squad which was playing in a tournament out in Nairobi.

During the past couple of seasons or so, I have had to battle to win a first-team place, because of the tremendous amount of talent there is at Elland-road. There was even talk at one stage last season that I might be allowed to go, in a player-exchange deal, but I still cannot say I have wanted to leave Leeds.

You see, a few seasons ago, I broke a leg, and that involved another sort of battle—a battle for fitness. When you're just starting to make your way in the game, and you get an injury like that, it frightens you, because you wonder if you will ever recover full form and fitness. I can only say that everyone at Leeds went out of their way to encourage me and help me regain both. And during the latter part of last season, I'm thankful to say, I really seemed to find my shooting boots again.

When I think back now, it seems a long time since I first came south—as, indeed, it is, comparatively speaking. I had chances to sign for other clubs, but Leeds won, in the end. Elsewhere in this book, you will read how Leeds manager Don Revie got picked up for speeding on his way to sign me. In fact, it surprised me more than a little, all that hustle! It was after 3 a.m. when I got to bed, and Don Revie was on his way back to Leeds, with the signing safely completed. But I'll say this for him—he earned that signature. Apart from his hurried long-distance trip to make sure of signing me, he had had my name in his notebook before any other manager. Leeds, you see, had spotted me when I was playing for Stobswell School, Dundee, before I had even played for the town team, let alone Scotland Boys! So Leeds won the race because they were first on the scene, and because they didn't forget, and because they were persistent. If a club can take all that trouble about an unknown youngster, that club must be something rather special. And Leeds are, as I've found out.

People have referred to the fact that I possess an explosive shot. Well, I have to confess that I've no idea how I happen to have this ability to crack a ball so hard. I was nick-named 'Hot-shot Lorimer' at school, but I guess I've been lucky to have been born with that instinctive ability, which doesn't even really need practice. The secret must lie in perfect timing, and I'm fortunate that I can hit the ball spot-on.

Footballers certainly didn't run in the family, really—an uncle of mine used to play for Lincoln City, but though the rest of the family played Soccer, there wasn't anyone else who came near to making the grade at League level. My Dad encouraged me, right enough, but when I look back, somehow it's always my mother I think of, for she was the one who had to keep my kit clean, when I was playing two games a day, every Saturday! In the morning, I played for the school; and in the afternoon, for the local youth club. And while we're on the subject of kit, I must admit that I think it's important for youngsters to be properly turned out. The feeling that you look the part can go a long way towards giving you the confidence you need, whether it's for football or for any other job of work.

Goals give me kicks, I won't deny that. And the game that sticks in my memory is the one in which I scored a hat-trick against Bury. I won't ever forget that one, it was an F.A. Cup-tie. Another game which evokes memories is one against Sheffield United—yes, that's the one in which I broke a leg. It was an F.A. Youth Cup match.

I had had three or four first-team games, and I was just beginning to think of myself as a budding star when ... wham! I broke a leg. And at 17, on the very threshold of your career, a broken leg can be a shattering experience, psychologically, as well as physically.

It meant that I had to start all over again. My leg was in plaster for six weeks; and then came five months of grinding, slogging work before I won my way back through the junior and reserve teams. As Eddie Gray says, and he should know, such an injury can be a terrific blow to your confidence. But I'm glad to be able to say that today, I don't even think about the injury when I go out on the park. In any case, they tell me that when a broken bone has knit together, it's thicker and tougher than it was before!

Memory No. 3 is that League Cup triumph at Wembley. For some reason, I'd dreamed of playing there, even as a kid; and even more than playing at Hampden Park. So it was a fabulous thrill for me to take part in such an important showgame, before 100,000 people, and walk off, knowing I was one of the 11 players who would collect a winner's medal. Now I've one ambition left—at least, one major ambition: and that's to play in a full international Scotland against England, with Scotland beating the auld enemy on her own ground, at Wembley!

18. *Those G.C.E. exams were worth it*

ROD BELFITT

MANY YOUNGSTERS THESE days face a problem when they have to decide about trying to make the grade in professional football, a problem which I had to tackle myself. Make no mistake about it, I wanted to become a footballer, and just after I left school in my native Doncaster, I went down to Highbury, to try my luck with Arsenal. But I found that I could not settle down in the south, and soon I was on my travels ... to Retford Town. From there, it was Elland-road next stop.

The problem which nagged at me, of course, was what would happen, if I didn't make the grade in professional Soccer? And as time went by, I realised that it could be only to my benefit if I continued with my studies, when I wasn't required for training. As a result, I became a part-time student at Doncaster Technical College, and eventually I sat for my G.C.E. examinations. It gave me a more secure feeling about plunging into the game, knowing that I would have other qualifications to fall back on, should things go wrong.

Once I had got those exams out of the way, of course, I was able to concentrate on football full-time, and although I'm now in my early 20's, I feel the extra effort of taking those exams was worth it, for I'm still young enough to 'come good', as they say, in League Soccer.

Indeed, I believe I have helped to play my part in the Leeds United success story, and I have played plenty of first-team games. Oddly enough, the highlight of my career so far came in the season Leeds *didn't* win the Inter-Cities Fairs Cup, but it was memorable for me, because although we lost in the final against Dinamo Zagreb, I certainly helped Leeds to get there—by scoring a hat-trick in the Elland-road leg of the semi-final against Kilmarnock. It was the first hat-trick in my senior career, and I'm hoping it won't be the last!

19. Split pants knocked United out of the Cup

SOCCER PLAYERS AND managers have their superstitions, just like anyone else. And if you believe in omens, you will believe that a split pair of pants knocked Leeds United out of the F.A. Cup last season. Believe it or not, this is what happened.

Don Revie had a lucky blue suit. He had worn it on match days for more than two years. The suit went with him to Budapest, when Leeds triumphed over Ferencvaros to win the Inter-Cities Fairs Cup; it went with him to Wembley, when Leeds beat Arsenal to carry off the Football League Cup; it went with him on every Soccer safari in Western Europe, and, with Revie and Leeds United, it penetrated the Iron Curtain, too.

On the day of the third-round F.A. Cup replay against Sheffield Wednesday at Elland-road, Don took out the lucky blue suit, and started to get dressed. There was a rending, tearing sound, and the seam of the trousers split. So Leeds United's manager had to change to a grey suit, and Wednesday won the replay, 3–1. Don admits: 'Sure, I'm superstitious—that's why I wore the lucky blue suit. See what happened when it came apart!' And this vein of superstition runs right through the Leeds United team.

The players at Elland-road reckon that following a particular routine before a game increases their confidence which explains, partly, why Jackie Charlton turned in the captaincy, because he likes to be last out on the field. And the skipper should be the leader. Jackie has another superstition. Before every game, during the kickabout, he belts the ball into the empty net. The players all say that he never risks his shot from further out than a couple of yards, in case he misses.

Jackie is known to his team-mates as Fred. The reason being that he once started to tell a story involving a character called Fred. The story was complicated, and by the time that Jackie was through telling it, every one of his listeners had stolen softly away. To this day, at Elland-road, no one knows what happened to Fred, the fellow who fell down the hole. But everyone calls Jackie Charlton Fred.

Today, Billy Bremner is the skipper of Leeds, and before every game he straps his ankle up in a special way. Nothing to do with it being sore, or tender, simply another Leeds superstition. There is another ritual to be gone through, too, as he leaves the dressing-room. Norman Hunter must hand the ball to him, to carry out on the field. Billy, of the fiery red head and pale complexion, is known to his team-mates as Chalky. No explanation needed here. As for Norman Hunter, they call him Tarz, short for Tarzan, whom, the lads claim, he resembles when he goes into a head-on tackle. Not for nothing is Norman known as Tarz—he's one of the hardest players in the game.

Goalkeeper Gary Sprake, of the fair hair and elegant build, is known as Ken, after comedian Ken Dodd. Because, although Gary's hair is blond, when he's doing his act, it sticks up just like Doddy's. Gary has his own superstition. He always has a massage from Les Cocker before a match.

No one seems to know why Paul Reaney is known as Ra-Ra, but everyone does know that he insists on being third in line, when the players go on to the field. Terry Cooper, they call him simply by his initials, T.C., always has a rub in the small of the back from Don Revie as he departs for the playing pitch.

SPLIT PANTS KNOCKED UNITED OUT OF CUP

Mike O'Grady is nick-named Shady, not because of any criminal tendencies, but because it's rhyming slang for his surname. Mike, Peter Lorimer and Eddie Gray say they are *not* superstitious, and don't do 'anything daft'. But Peter Lorimer is known as Lash, because of the way he can belt a football goalwards. Eddie Gray's nick-name is Chucky, which goes back to the early days, when Billy Bremner, a fellow-Scot and an old hand, used this as a pet name to make Eddie feel at home at Elland-road. Mick Jones is known by two names—Jonah, and M.I. Jonah is merely a play on his surname, and the M.I. bit comes from the first two letters of his christian name.

Johnny Giles gets both Farmer and Paddy, dependent on who is talking to him. He walks around in his jock-strap all the while he is getting ready for the game. That's the first thing he puts on. Then come stockings, boots and jersey and last of all, shorts. The order is always the same.

Paul Madeley is known to his team-mates as Big Ed, not a corruption of Big 'ead, but after the talking horse in the T.V. series. The lads say Paul speaks slowly and precisely, just like Big Ed, in fact. Terry Hibbitt, whose second christian name is Arthur, is called, simply, Arth. His superstition is simple, too—before every game, he rubs his chest and legs with a well-known inhalant.

Mick Bates is short and muscular, hence his nick-name of Chunky. And Albert Johanneson, who is a big favourite with all his team-mates at Elland-road, comes in for the affectionate tag of Jo-Jo, while Rod Belfitt is known as Blisters. It seems that during a round of golf at Scarborough last season, Rod's feet became blistered. So he took off his shoes and socks, and finished the round in his bare feet.

So the next time you watch the Leeds lads run on the pitch, you can go through the team and recall just what routines they have been going through, a few minutes earlier. And if you really want to be familiar, you can call them by their aliases.

20. *The Team behind the Team*

KEITH ARCHER

As GENERAL MANAGER of Leeds United, I am told that I am the youngest in the Football League, I suppose you could call me the Billy Bremner of the Elland-road administrative team. The skipper of the small band of dedicated people who keep the wheels turning in the office.

Everyone has heard of the hard, unrelenting work which goes on on the playing side of the club and it is probably not my place to tell you that there is not a man from our manager Don Revie to the youngest apprentice who is not prepared to give his 'lot' for Leeds United. But here and now I would like to put in a word for the unsung lads, and lasses, of my back-room team.

The magnificent achievements of Billy and his merry men have brought us all great pleasure and satisfaction. They have also brought a load of problems as far as we are concerned.

We welcome them and there is not a single member of my six-strong team of full-timers, and the many part-timers who help out at rush periods, who would not be willing to work night and day to play a part in keeping the club in the forefront of the battle for the game's top honours.

A collection of individuals gets nowhere in the game today and team spirit is just as essential on our side as it is among the players. We all have our separate jobs to do but the smooth running of the administrative machine depends

THE TEAM BEHIND THE TEAM

on the way everybody 'mucks in' when the difficulties seem almost unsurmountable.

Like the team on the field, we cannot win every time. But just like the players we never stop learning. And I can assure every Leeds United fan that our aim is to give you the kind of top-class service you are entitled to expect from one of the best clubs in the world.

The administration involved in a club like United, with its commitments not only in Britain, but in Europe and behind the Iron Curtain, is tremendous. I certainly did not realise the enormity of the task which faced me when I decided to pack up my job in Insurance just before the start of the 1967–68 season and join the Elland-road staff.

Friends and acquaintances congratulated me, and meant it, on landing a job in which I could do much as I pleased for the whole of the summer. They did not know the half of it. But, believe me, I soon found out, for in that first season in the 'hot-seat' Leeds United took part in 66 competitive games, over half of which were staged at Elland-road.

Besides dealing with the day to day running of the club, our morning's mail can include everything from a directive from the Football Association or the Football League to requests for autographs and even letters asking what size of football boots Jack Charlton plays in, it meant a terrific build-up of pressure on the office staff.

Board meetings, at which I must be in attendance, had to be held, wages had to be paid, playing staff problems about such things as housing and accommodation had to be solved, travelling arrangements to countries all over Europe had to be spot on. All the scores of everyday problems which face a successful club these days had to be dealt with.

And on top of all this the thousands of extra tickets for the big games had to be allocated and sold with at least three would-be spectators clamouring for every single one.

Then there were the regular and prolonged conferences with the Police on how best to deal with the crowd problem and especially the small minority who, at every club, seem to be intent on making everyone's job twice as difficult. We can well do without them at Elland-road.

The age-old problem of how to get a quart into a pint pot was with us day and night and while I am the first to admit that we could not satisfy everyone, we could not have got through as well as we did without the forebearance of the great majority of Leeds fans.

No one knows better than I do that we did not please all the people all the time, and I hope that this brief insight into some of our trials and tribulations will help the few who found fault to better understand our problems and to help them to be more patient.

Since I was thrown in at the deep end there has been very little opportunity to relax as the club has gone from success to success. In last summer's 'rest period', for example we sold a record number of season tickets which brought in well over £100,000 of essential revenue.

That was in a 12-week spell in which preparations for the playing season, and everything its fixtures entailed at home and abroad, had to go on all the while.

No doubt we will continue to make mistakes, but I feel that we have come a long way in a short time, thanks to the magnificent spirit which exists, as it does everywhere else, under the big stand at Elland-road.

And our prime objective is to make the back-room team just as professional and efficient as the men Don Revie sends out to do battle against the world's top opposition. I am sure that our fans would not ask for more.

21. Elland Road Academy

LEEDS UNITED is not just another football club, it is an academy of Soccer sciences. There are others, of course—Old Trafford, Maine-road, Anfield, Goodison, White Hart-lane, Stamford Bridge. But Leeds can claim, with perfect truth, that their Soccer academy is as good as any, and better than most. After all, it has taken several years to develop, and there has been much thought and effort put into the running of it.

The academy has its head—Don Revie. And its backroom boys. Any leader will tell you that he is only as good as his team, and this applies off the field, as well as on it. The secret lies in hand-picking the best men for the jobs needed doing. Don Revie has been fortunate and skilful in the job of hand-picking his backroom team. And today the results and the rewards are showing through.

There is MAURICE LINDLEY, Keighley-born, who played with Town Boys and then joined Barnoldswick Town in the Yorkshire League, as an amateur. At 17, he moved on to Merseyside, as a part-time professional with Everton; he stayed there for 17 years. He was a contemporary of men like Warney Cresswell and Dixie Dean, Joe Mercer, Tommy Lawton, Cliff Britton, Ted Sagar, and Everton's manager today, Harry Catterick. Maurice Lindley had a special pal in Tommy Jones, Everton's Welsh international centre-half.

In 1953, Maurice moved on to Swindon Town, as manager there; and a couple of years later he became secretary-manager of Barry Town, in the Welsh League.

This job occupied him for several months, then he went as secretary-manager to Crewe, where he stayed two years, and then he joined the staff at Elland-road, as coach. But he didn't stay, for Maurice moved across to Sheffield Wednesday, in a similar capacity, only to return, finally to Leeds as chief scout under Don Revie. And two years ago, he became assistant manager at Elland-road.

In his new career with Leeds he has travelled hundreds of thousands of miles, at home and abroad. He has followed up scouting reports, and watched hundreds of youngsters, to see for himself if they are likely to measure up to the exacting standards Leeds set. And it has been part of his job to assess the playing opponents of Leeds United, in Europe as well as England. His companion on these European safaris is usually coach Syd Owen, who several years ago turned down the chance of a good job at Tottenham, in order to see the job through at Elland-road. That's the sort of club loyalty Leeds expect, and breed.

Maurice recalls one of his more unusual trips, when he says: 'Once, I went to Las Palmas, in the Canary Islands, not for the holiday, but to watch Valencia in a game. It was our only possible chance to assess them, before Leeds played them in a Fairs Cities Cup match. It was one of the few occasions I was on my own, too, and didn't I know it, when I got there!

'We had sent several letters and cables from Elland-road, to say that I would be going out for the game. But when I arrived, there was no one to meet me, and I found it impossible to get to see anyone in authority, no matter what I tried.

'Eventually, I had to buy a ticket for the game on the local black market—it cost well over the odds, but it was the only way I could get to see the game, it appeared, and I finished up with a seat in the stand.

'Not exactly the sort of thing you anticipate when you go on a scouting mission such as this. At Leeds, for instance, we do everything possible to make visitors welcome and see

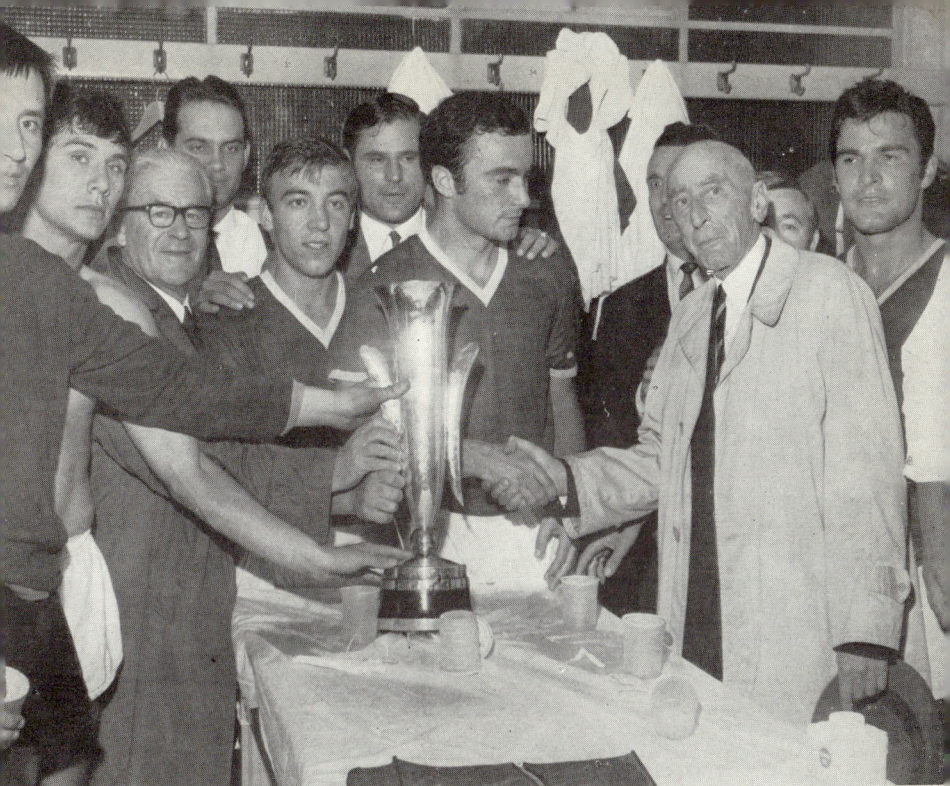

ABOVE: Former Leeds United chairman, the late Albert Morris, congratulates members of the Dinamo Zagreb team after they had won the 1967 Fairs Cup. They beat United 2–0 over the two legs.

Billy Bremner rejoices in characteristic fashion after scoring the winning goal against Standard Liège in last season's Inter-Cities Fairs Cup.

ABOVE: Mick Jones puts the ball over the line for the goal which brought the Inter-Cities Fairs Cup to Leeds. Jack Charlton, who headed the ball down from a corner, watches anxiously as Jones succeeds in scoring the only goal of the tie. BELOW: The Inter-Cities Fairs Cup in Leeds at last. *left to right*: Syd Owen, Maurice Lindley, Don Revie, Les Cocker, Bob English and Cyril Partridge.

that they have every facility. However, my experience wasn't quite so bad as one which Syd Owen had, when he went out to Spain to run the rule over Valencia. Another season, Syd didn't even manage to get a stand seat—he finished up standing right at the back of the terraces, surrounded by a mob of almost hysterical Spanish fans.'

There are times when you have to be up early to get the signature of some promising youngster whose name is pencilled down in the books of more than one club. Time you have to stay up late, to accomplish the mission, too. Maurice recalls his most memorable signing trip, as being the one on which he accompanied manager Don Revie to Scotland. They had been tipped off that they might be pipped in their bid to land young Peter Lorimer, so they immediately set out from Leeds. It was after 8 p.m.

Peter had left school that same day, and from then on, it could be a battle between several clubs. Leeds aimed to be first in, and successful, too. Maurice and Don sped through the night on their signing mission, and they were in such a hurry to get there that they got picked up for speeding through Perth! When they arrived in Dundee, it was 1.30 in the morning, but they didn't dally. Straight down to business it was, and by the time they left, at 3 a.m., they had Peter Lorimer's signature. They even had the Press there, to take a picture of the signing, and then the Leeds pair turned and headed for home.

Maurice has spotted and landed some fine young Soccer talent for Leeds. And the one he reckons will turn out to be best of all is Eddie Gray. 'I honestly believe Eddie can be the best player to come out of Scotland,' says Maurice. 'Plenty of players have gone before him, and won football fame—our own Billy Bremner, for instance, but for my money, Eddie Gray is nowhere near his full potential yet. And when he does reach his peak, he'll be one of the greats. That's the most gratifying thing about the whole job, you know—you spot a lad, a raw youngster, really, you take him to Leeds, hand him over to Syd Owen and trainer Les Cocker, and, as the time passes, see how the youngster has been moulded so that he finally breaks through and makes the grade at top level. It's tremendously satisfying, when that happens, and you know you played an initial part in it.'

When Don Revie bowed out of the spotlight linking his name with Manchester United and Italy, a few months ago, he said quite simply that he wanted to stay and finish the job with Leeds, to make Leeds United the *new* Manchester United, in fact. And he referred to Leeds as 'one great family'. He wasn't being flippant; he was in deadly earnest. For that is how Leeds like to regard themselves, and everyone connected with them. 'We're all part of a family' is the creed. And it has worked so well, for it has encouraged everyone to have pride in the club, it has fostered that intangible thing called team spirit, on and off the field.

This team-spirit training comes right at the start. Maurice Lindley has talked about seeing a raw youngster break through to the top. But how does it all begin, when a lad joins Leeds straight from home?

He probably signs as an apprentice professional, around the age of 15. And the regulars—Don Revie, Maurice Lindley, Syd Owen, Bob English (second team trainer and physiotherapist), Cyril Patridge (who is in charge of the youth team) and Les Cocker are always on hand, to advise and help. In addition, the youngster can count on guidance from a retired Leeds headmaster and a clergyman. The lad will also have good digs with a 'foster-mother'. Everything is done to make him feel at home, straight away.

Even before the lad arrives at Leeds, United officials have visited his parents and explained what lies ahead for their son. And they give the parents 'nothing but the truth', as they explain what a footballing career with Leeds United will mean.

Hard work, complete dedication, clean living, early-to-bed hours and so on. The lad himself is also invited to visit Elland-road, first, so that he can judge for himself if

ELLAND ROAD ACADEMY

he is likely to like the life there. And if he thinks the life there is for him, and he usually does, he becomes an apprentice professional for three years. At the end of that period, assuming he has shown enough talent, he can negotiate his terms with the club as a full-time professional.

Maurice Lindley doesn't wrap it up, when he says: 'It's a hard apprenticeship, right enough. The hours at the ground can be long, and the jobs the lads have to do can be tedious. For while they're learning to play football, they're also cleaning the boots of the established players and doing all sorts of other more or less menial tasks. There's no room or time for a lad to get big-headed, but all the time, the accent is on building character.'

The Leeds 'landladies' are vetted closely; and United lay down keen terms under which the youngsters are to be brought up as part of the family. It's not so much a case of going into digs, in fact, as going to a home from home.

At 15, as an apprentice professional, a lad draws about £7 a week. Not a fortune. At 17, in the last year of his apprenticeship, his pay has risen to £9 in the close season, £10 in the playing season. And then, once he turns full-time professional, he can earn as much as his talent commands.

Leeds look at other aspects, apart from the footballing side. For example, apprentice professionals are taught the value of money.

Each apprentice professional has a bank book, but Leeds United keep it for him, and from his weekly pay they deduct a sum which they put into his bank account. If the lad wishes to draw out some cash, he has to have a good reason, and he's got to spell it out to the club officials.

The apprentice professional eats well, but simply. His food is closely supervised, to ensure that he gets a varied and balanced diet. The sort of food that will do him good, in fact. And there are regular medical checks by the club doctor Ian Adams, to ensure that he is making satisfactory progress physically.

There are sex talks for the lads, too—usually this task

falls to trainer Les Cocker, who doesn't mince his words. It's his job to see that every lad knows about the pitfalls which can await the young and unworldly, and the glamour surrounding professional footballers increases with growing fame. So right from the start, lads are taught to beware the temptations of loose living. The club padre, the Rev. John Jackson, travels from York to Leeds once a week to give the lads guidance, and former headmaster Mr. Jeffrey Sanders is on hand to advise lads about courses they can take, to ensure that they have something to fall back on, once their playing days are over.

Plenty of lads at Leeds attend classes during the day and in the evenings, commerce and trade come into the syllabus, and there is a watchful eye kept on their leisure pursuits, to make sure they don't go 'off the rails'.

In short, Leeds United do everything humanly possible to see that each lad who arrives at Elland-road is treated as one of the sons in a large family. Leeds want to bring their lads up right, and they take tremendous time and trouble to ensure that they do.

Their reward, in one way, often comes from the parents of lads themselves, who write to the club expressing appreciation of all that Leeds have done for their sons. Inevitably, some of the boys who set out with Soccer stars in their eyes just do not make it, not everyone can be a success, and, of course, these boys move out of the game or on to other clubs, maybe in a lower and less demanding sphere.

But even then, their parents often write to Leeds, to say a special 'Thank you'. Maurice Lindley says: 'It's always hard to have to tell a youngster that we don't think he is going to make the grade, after all. But the blow for us is often softened by the letter from his parents, after he has left. Many a time we have had such letters. The parents express their thanks to the club, for the way they have looked after the youngster during his apprenticeship at Leeds. And this encourages us to go on looking after lads, being ever careful about their welfare for when they

ELLAND ROAD ACADEMY

do depart, they make the name of Leeds United known around the country, as a club which really cares about *everyone* in the family.'

And, having emphasised once more that there is this tremendous family spirit at Leeds, let's bring in two more senior members. With Maurice Lindley, they make up a formidable trio ... and around the club they are known as The Three Musketeers. So step up, SYD OWEN and LES COCKER.

These two just have to be bracketed together, because there is a heart-warming story about how they came to join forces, in the first place. Syd Owen, of course, was famous as Luton Town's long-serving centre-half; indeed, he was the barrier which many a goal-scoring centre-forward found impassable. Syd shared in the glory of a Cup-final appearance for Luton, and when he hung up his playing boots, he became Town's manager.

Syd decided that he wanted a first-team trainer, so, as often happens, the club advertised the job. And again, as so often happens in football, when a job is going, there were plenty of applicants. Les Cocker was one of those applicants. Now Les was a completely unknown quantity to Luton and Syd Owen—in fact, although Les had played for a Northern club called Accrington Stanley, Syd admits: 'I'd never even heard of him!'

Les, of course, didn't realise that and, even if he had, it wouldn't have daunted him when he wrote to Luton seeking the trainer's job. But when Syd Owen read Les Cocker's letter, he decided to look no further for a trainer. 'This is the man for me,' he decided, at once.

What made Les Cocker's letter so special? What could there possibly have been in it, that convinced Syd Owen that Cocker was the right man for the job? Let Syd tell the story: 'The first thing that impressed me, and I can still visualise it now, was the firmness of his handwriting. I sensed that here was a fellow who knew his own mind, who believed in himself, who put his heart into the words he wrote. That handwriting was like the man himself—unshakeable. It simply *oozed* character.

'And the letter itself made no bones about the writer's faith in his own ability. The words said, boldly and clearly, exactly how he would do the job of a trainer. They listed his qualifications. They were crisp and concise. In effect, they said that Cocker knew he would be a success in the job. All he required was the chance to prove it to Luton Town. So I replied immediately, and invited him for an interview. It was a foregone conclusion, really—Les Cocker had landed himself the job even before he knocked on the door. And when we did meet, face to face, and talked about the game, and how we felt about it, that was it. I just told him that he could consider himself Luton Town's trainer, and all that was left was one more question. When could he start?'

So the team of Owen and Cocker came into being. Later, Luton and Syd Owen parted company, but Cocker stayed on for a while. Yet Syd Owen never forgot the man he had left behind and almost as soon as he had joined Leeds, who were looking for a trainer, as well as a coach, Syd mentioned Les Cocker's name. Within a short time, the two men were working side by side again, this time at Elland-road.

Now let Syd Owen take up the story. He says: 'I was born in Birmingham, so when I decided to become a professional footballer, it was only natural that I should sign for the St. Andrews club. That was in 1945, just after I had come out of the R.A.F.

'Harry Storer was the Birmingham manager in those days and, believe me, he was a hard man. He wasn't unfair at all, but he did believe in letting his players know that they were expected to work at their job all the time. And there was no such thing as taking a breather during a game, so far as Harry was concerned. He believed that football was a game of physical contact, which it most certainly is, and that victory went to the brave.

ELLAND ROAD ACADEMY

'Probably it was Harry Storer who first brought it home to me that Soccer is a man's game—a game in which you have to be prepared to go for the half-chance. Leeds United have been accused in the past of being a dirty side, but that just isn't true. We are a hard side, and I don't see that there is anything to be ashamed of, in admitting that. I know plenty of managers who wish that their players had the same sort of spirit as all our players have.'

Syd wasn't long with Birmingham, as it happened. And after a season there, he was transfer-listed at £1,500. And what a bargain fee that turned out to be for Luton Town, who signed him! Syd stayed as a player with Luton until 1959, when they went to Wembley in the F.A. Cup, and lost a dramatic final against Nottingham Forest by the odd goal in three.

Syd says: 'Only the season before our Wembley run, I had decided to hang up my boots; but the Luton directors asked me to stay on, until a replacement had been found. I decided to give it another season and look what happened. I finished up being voted Player of the Year! That Cup final was my last game for Luton, and although we lost, the honour I won was some compensation for the disappointment of defeat in the game itself. Strangely enough, at one time Leeds United had three men on the payroll who had been voted Player of the Year, in various seasons. There was myself, there was Don Revie, and then came Bobby Collins. And then Jackie Charlton followed it up.'

When Syd finished playing for Luton, he didn't finish his service there, because he took over as team manager, when Dally Duncan departed for Blackburn. But after less than a season, Syd resigned. A month later, he received a telegram which was to change his career completely. The telegram came from Leeds, then managed by Jack Taylor, and it offered Syd a job at Elland-road as chief coach. He's been there ever since.

Don Revie was still a Leeds player, in fact, when Syd and Les Cocker teamed up again, at Elland-road. But with

Don's guiding hand, and the tremendous backing from Maurice Lindley, Syd Owen and Les Cocker, Leeds have gone from strength to strength. Syd says: 'It's true that I could have gone to Tottenham, as assistant to manager Bill Nicholson; and there have been offers to me from several other clubs, who wanted me as manager. But each time I thought of how hard we had worked to get Leeds going, and each time I felt convinced that we were on the point of reaping the rewards for all the work that had been put in. And I've never regretted my decision to stay at Elland-road.'

It's not just a question of material success, with Syd Owen. For he adds: 'So long as I can take an active part in the day-to-day affairs of the club, which means being out on the park with the players, this is the job I want to do. I don't want to be cooped up in an office, chained to a desk.

'It has taken 10 years to build this family atmosphere at Leeds and we neither need nor make apology for referring to it as such, for it is something in which we strongly believe. Now I am convinced that the future at Elland-road is brighter than ever before. In some ways, I regard myself as a professor of Soccer, teaching the players the arts and skills of the greatest sport in the world. I get a tremendous amount of satisfaction from passing on all I have learned myself, and from teaching the lads what hard work alone is worth. For make no mistake, hard work is demanded, and you can accomplish a hell of a lot with it.

'Football skills are instinctive, to a large extent. But you can help a player to develop his skills, and make the best use of them. When it comes to working them hard, as well, I regard this as an important part of character building. After all, it doesn't say a lot for anyone if they're bone idle. And no Leeds player is ever encouraged to slack.

'Another side of my job, over the years, has been to watch and analyse opponents we have been due to play, all over Europe. Maurice Lindley has mentioned the problems we've had, on some of our trips. When I went to watch

ELLAND ROAD ACADEMY

Valencia, in fact, I found that through some slip-up, no ticket had been arranged for me, and I finished up doing a deal with the hall porter at my hotel. He managed to get a ticket for me, on the black market.

'Even then, my troubles were far from over. I'd got a ticket, all right, but when I got to the turnstile where I was supposed to gain admittance, I found it closed. I couldn't get into the stand, despite all my efforts, and I finally ended up "talking" my way in sign language on to the terraces. I'd got a job to do, and I had to find a way of making sure that I did it—it was as simple as that. In Soccer, as in other walks of life, you must use initiative and improvise, when things don't go smoothly, or when the chance occurs. That's one of the things I stress to the lads who play for Leeds, Soccer isn't a blackboard game, things go wrong, and the unexpected happens. When things are not going right on the field, you've got to take swift stock of the situation and improvise.'

In his 10 years at Leeds, Syd Owen has personally helped to groom almost every youngster on the books. Only three players, in fact, have not passed through his hands—Mick Jones, Johnny Giles and Mike O'Grady. And they were ready-made, expensive signings. Soccer is Syd Owen's hobby, as well as his work. His whole life, virtually. 'I work at some aspect of the game from Monday to Saturday, often late at night,' he says. 'And during the season, I see a game somewhere or other almost every Sunday. It means that I don't have much home life the greater part of the year. But Soccer is an exacting taskmaster, if you aim to do the job properly. And I do.'

Now come in, LES COCKER, who was born in Stockport, and started out as an amateur footballer who was learning to become a painter and decorator, when he went into the Army as an 18-year-old. He played for Stockport County whenever he got leave, and turned his back on the painting and decorating to become a full-time professional footballer, when he was demobbed. From 1945 to 1951, he was a Stockport player; and he played in every position except centre-half and goal. They still remember his fearless style at Edgeley Park, especially as a centre-forward, which was where he played most of his games.

Les moved on, finally, from Stockport to ill-fated Accrington Stanley, where he stayed until 1959. By then, he had become interested in the coaching side of the game, and for four years he had held the full F.A. coaching badge. Many players take the preliminary part of the test, then neglect to qualify as a full coach; but Les Cocker and others have proved convincingly that the time and effort are well worth while.

Les says: 'I had determined to prepare myself for the day I had to quit playing, and that day comes to every footballer, if he faces up to the realities of life. Age catches up with everyone. When Syd Owen asked me to join him on the staff at Luton, I snapped up the chance, and I've blessed that day many times since, for when we teamed up together, it was the start of a partnership which has lasted for years.

'Those who still remain sceptical about coaching are missing out. When Walter Winterbottom was the England team manager, I got my first chance to learn how things go at representative level, for I became trainer to the England Under-23 side against Israel. Since then, I've worked under Billy Wright, Joe Mercer and John Harris, when they were the managers in charge of Under-23 teams, and I've learned something from every one of them. You never stop learning, in this game. And one of the greatest honours which has come my way was when Sir Alf Ramsey and Harold Shepherdson called on me to help them in preparing the England squad for the 1966 World Cup. That's something I'll *never* forget.

'When I said you are always learning, if you are prepared to take the time and the trouble, I meant it. For even a full F.A. coaching badge isn't the be-all and end-all of things. For instance, I've taken a three-year F.A. course on the treatment of injuries, another aspect of the game, and in the afternoons at Elland-road, I spend time helping Bob English in the treatment room.

'With our experience and qualifications, Syd Owen and I can interchange duties, but my main responsibility is to ensure that the players of Leeds United are fit. And I don't think anyone will argue that they're not! Physical fitness is regarded, and rightly so, as being of extreme importance, and my job is to make sure that the first teamers are 100 per cent up to the demands of 90 punishing minutes on a match day. Syd is responsible for the tactical approach to a game, and between us we try to adapt the tactics to the talent at our disposal at Elland-road. So we try to pick the best out of everything we see, at world-class level, never mind club level, and utilise it all for the benefit of Leeds United. It's paid off handsomely, as our results over the past seasons show.

'And there is one more basic for success—loyalty. Maurice Lindley was 17 years with Everton; Syd Owen was at Luton almost the whole of his playing career; I was with Stockport and Accrington. We all learned the lesson that a player must be loyal to his club, and we have applied that lesson at Leeds. I think we have succeeded, pretty well, too.'

Of course, Leeds have a prolific stream of young talent coming off the assembly line. Any club must groom youngsters, all the time, if it wishes to have a steady supply ready to step into the first team. And Leeds United set great store by their youngsters—yes, even the lads whose names are not widely known to the Soccer-going public. Yet....

CYRIL PATRIDGE, Yorkshire-born but a Queen's Park Rangers player for a long time, takes charge of the youth team, and he says: 'One of the things which struck me forcibly, when I arrived at Leeds, was that many of the kids never got anywhere near representing their country, as schoolboy footballers. Yet they are well on the way to making the grade in top-class professional Soccer.'

Cyril lists youngsters who have come up through the junior sides, after having joined United straight from school, and now they have already a fair amount of first-team experience.

There is wing-half Jimmy Lumsden, aged 20, who played for Glasgow Boys; Swansea-born Terry Yorath, who did play for Swansea and Wales schoolboys, and at 18 has won Under-23 honours; inside-forward Mick Bates, aged 20, of Doncaster and Yorkshire boys; left-winger Terry Hibbitt, aged 21, who played for Bradford boys.

There is goalkeeper David Harvey, aged 21, whom manager Don Revie rates in the Gary Sprake class. David played for Leeds schoolboys, and asked for a move because he was unsettled, not surprisingly, in view of the fact that his first-team chances have been so limited, with Gary Sprake around.

Then there is utility defender Nigel Davey, aged 23, who never played for anyone but his local school team at Great Preston, near Leeds. These lads follow in the footsteps of the regular first-team members who joined United straight from school.

Leeds have never rushed into the signing market, even though they have paid huge fees for players like Mick Jones and the legendary John Charles. Indeed, the first-teamers today are home-produced, with but three exceptions. Mick Jones cost £100,000 when he was signed from Sheffield United; Johnny Giles cost around £40,000 when he arrived from Manchester United; and Mike O'Grady cost something like £30,000 when he was signed from Huddersfield Town. If you want to add to the bill, of course, you can include the cost of one air fare, which brought Albert Johanneson from South Africa to Elland-road.

Up-and-coming youngsters will soon be pressing for first-team places, too, for the Leeds academy is grooming fresh talent all the time. For example, there are four teenagers who could be making their mark on the game within a couple of seasons—don't forget that Leeds believe if they're good enough, they're old enough.

There is 17-year-old Chris Galvin, a left-winger or left-half, from Huddersfield Boys; there is centre-forward Bob Malt, also just 17—he hails from the North-East, and is rated to be the double in looks and style of Jimmy Greenhoff, for whom Birmingham City paid Leeds a £70,000 fee; and there is Doncaster Boys centre-half Jack Kennedy, aged 18.

Following closely behind these youngsters are half a dozen apprentice professionals, all aiming to make the breakthrough with Leeds into First Division football. Perhaps top of the list is Carlisle and England Boys inside-right Bobby Rutherford, but if you're looking for someone in the middle line, you might take Neath and Wales centre-half Keith Edwards, a 16-year-old with tremendous potential; and you can add the names of 15-year-old Rotherham Boys inside-forward Brian Stuart, North Derbyshire Boys right-winger Peter Earnshaw, aged 17, 15-year-old inside-forward Jimmy Mann, from Goole Boys, Colin Smith, aged 16, wing-half of Bishop Auckland and Durham Boys, and Stephen Brown, 16-year-old Leeds Boys wing-half or full-back.

It is well worth remembering, too, that United's South Wales scout, Jack Pickard, is still unearthing talent from over the Border. He sent John Charles and Gary Sprake to Leeds, in the first place, and he was also responsible for spotting Terry Yorath and Keith Edwards. Not a bad contribution towards the Leeds United success story!

This, then, is an insight into the backroom men who help to make Leeds United tick; an insight into the methods they use; an insight into the tremendous amount of thought and time put into the job. Leeds United, rightly, are proud of the Soccer talent they have produced at Elland-road. And they are confident that, while they might not scoop the pool every time, they get their fair share of the youngsters who will make the grade in the top flight, and Leeds believe they will go on unearthing and grooming such young talent for years to come. Thanks to The Three Musketeers, and the men who work with them, around the length and breadth of Britain.

22. *The Moment of Truth*

THE END OF season 1968–69 brought, at long last, what Leeds United had sought for season after season—undisputed recognition that they were the champions of England. And, more than that, worthy champions. The team of champion near-missers became the champion champions—by taking the First Division title by a record number of points. Sixty-seven. The highest total ever recorded in the history of the championship and the proof, in black and white, that Leeds were the most consistent team throughout the length and breadth of the country.

Manager Don Revie summed it up: 'We knew we were a great team, but we always had that feeling that we had to prove it to everyone else. And the title success proved our point. We lost only two games throughout the season, finished with an unbeaten run of 28 games. And we were finally after the European Cup.'

Four clubs battled for the championship throughout the season. They were Leeds, Liverpool, Everton and Arsenal. At one stage, the race belonged to anyone; at another, Liverpool were the club who seemed to be edging out in front; and then came the transformation. Liverpool lost ground, while Leeds carried on winning and drawing. And it was Leeds who opened up a five-point gap at the top.

Now it was Liverpool who were hanging on grimly, hoping that their rivals would make the slips which would enable them to overhaul Leeds. Around Easter, it became clear that the four-horse race was narrowing down to a two-horse race, as Everton and Arsenal faded somewhat, and began to fight their own private duel for the honour of finishing third.

As for Liverpool, they stuck to their task, and refused to concede that their title hopes had vanished. Even after Leeds had visited Highbury and beaten Arsenal 2-1, there was still hope in the Anfield camp. But now it rested mainly upon the fact that they had one game in hand on Leeds, and upon Everton, their deadly Merseyside rivals. For Leeds, having defeated Arsenal, had still to visit Goodison and Anfield.

The same night that Everton met Leeds, Liverpool played at Coventry—who were fighting for First Division survival. There was no quarter asked or given, in either match; and no score in either match, when the final whistle went. So Leeds had played 40 games, and collected 64 points; Liverpool had three matches to go, and had collected 59 points. And the Anfield battle was the one which could prove the decider. A point for Leeds there, and they knew the title belonged to them—it didn't matter, then, if they won, drew or lost at home to Nottingham Forest in their final game of the season. For Liverpool could not catch them.

It was a full house at Anfield, 53,750 folk inside the ground, 2,000 more locked out, when they closed the gates. A game vibrant with tension, with pulsating challenges as players went in for the ball without asking for quarter. A game with a few scoring chances, but a game without goals, after 90 minutes. Because Leeds, superbly disciplined in defence, could not be caught out once. And their last line of defence, Gary Sprake, made a magnificent save from Ian Callaghan, when it seemed as if Liverpool *might* just hold them up.

At the finale, the supporters of both teams rose to Leeds and, sportingly, the Liverpool players congratulated their opponents man for man. While the magnificent Kop gave the United team a standing ovation, as they completed a lap of honour. It was the culmination of years of planning by Leeds manager Don Revie and his men, years in which they had known the heartache of finishing second, second, fourth and fourth in the title quest; of getting nowhere in the League Cup—until that final victory against Arsenal; of going to Wembley itself in the F.A. Cup—and missing out there; and of finally lifting the Fairs Cities Cup, after a losing semi-final, and then a losing final.

Cold figures tell a fantastic story of the way Leeds United had plugged away at their eventual goal, the League championship. From the start of their promotion campaign which took them out of Division 2, they had played 341 matches, season by season, like this: 48, 52, 57, 63, 68, 53. They had won 194, drawn 87, and lost only 60. And with the final game, at home against Nottingham Forest only 48 hours after the epic duel at Anfield, Leeds proudly wrote another figure into the record books. For victory against Forest gave them a record total of 67 points for winning the title, one more than Arsenal or Tottenham, the previous joint holders, had achieved.

So now, where do Leeds go from here? There is but *one* way—forward. Into Europe, and then against the world. For there are always mountains to climb; and while Leeds have conquered three peaks, there is still the European Cup, and after that, the Everest of the world-club championship. Be sure that Leeds, still flushed with the triumph they scored last April at Anfield, and with the League trophy adding to the silverware on their sideboard, will not stand still. Relentlessly, they will be urged to go on, and on. Until there are no more honours to win.